When Women Work Together

When Women Work Together

Using Our Strengths
to Overcome
Our Challenges

Carolyn S. Duff
with Barbara Cohen, MA, LMFT

Conari Press
Berkeley, CA

Printed in the United States of America on recycled paper
Cover: Tom Morgan at Blue Design

ISBN: 0-943233-53-4

Library of Congress Cataloging-in-Publication Data

Duff, Carolyn S., 1941-
    When women work together : using our strengths to overcome our challenges / Carolyn S. Duff with Barbara Cohen.
        p. cm.
    Includes bibliographical references and index.
    ISBN 0-943233-53-4 (alk. paper) : $12.95
    1. Psychology, Industrial. 2. Interpersonal relations. 3. Women-Employment—Psychological aspects. I. Cohen, Barbara. II. Title.
HF5548.8.D784 1993   93-23771
158.7'082—dc20   CIP

To our mothers

Ruth M. Searing
and
C. Marion Cohen

for their love and support

Acknowledgments

We thank all the people in our lives who helped us create this book.

I would like to give special recognition and thanks to my partner Betty Brown for carrying our other business, BCA Resources, during the time I worked on this project. Betty modeled everything we say in this book about women supporting each other and cooperating toward mutual goals.

Also thanks and sincere appreciation to Gail Maloney who spent hours using her computer expertise to generate meaning from our 513 survey forms; to Ashley Ryan for her invaluable input and perceptive editing; to Christine Ferguson for her encouragement and challenging criticisms; to Judy Peterson for her patience and care with the magic of 5.1; to all the women who gave us their time, their stories, and their thoughtful insights as background for this book; and to Mary Jane Ryan for taking a chance and guiding me through the process.

All of us wish to thank Valerie Mauksch for scheduling the first WomenWorks workshop at Poudre Valley Hospital and the women who attended for convincing us women were ready to listen. Thank you to our families for their confidence and love. And, finally, to Marty Hook Gormally who believed in us and supported us from the start.

Carolyn S. Duff
Fort Collins, CO

Table of Contents

Common Problems and Strategies for Coping

The Future is Ours

Introduction

Today we have a critical mass of women poised to change the workplace forever. Women have entered the work force in unprecedented numbers, and we're not leaving. Not only are we penetrating the depths and rising to the heights of established professions and corporations, we are also starting our own businesses in record numbers. The Small Business Administration counts about five million women-owned businesses and predicts soon women will own nearly 40 percent of small businesses.

This means that women now work with women as often, if not more often, than we work with men. No matter where we work or what we do, however, we all have strong feelings about working together. Cynthia, a veteran of twenty-seven years working with and managing women within a major computer products company, sums up her experience by dividing women into two groups: those who work well together and those who create discomfort and conflict with one another. Sound familiar?

1

"The good ones," she says, "are open, honest, supportive, and caring. They perform with high competence,
assertiveness, and confidence in themselves and others. The
difficult women, the ones who cause tension and disrupt
group function, tend to be distant and aggressive, behind-
the-scene operators. They're sensitive to criticism, see other
women as rivals, and promote themselves at others' expense."

After five years of training women to work together, it
is my belief that we women do not need to be divided in this
way. We *can* learn to come together and work positively and
productively for a mutually beneficial future. *How* we work
together has always been important to women; but in the
downsized '90s, as workers generally are tending to receive
fewer gains in salary and status, a supportive environment
where women can function both productively and happily
together is more important than ever as one of the intangible
rewards of work.

That's why now is the time for women who work with
women to take a good long look at ourselves and our
relationships with one another. In doing so, we must not only
celebrate our strengths, but also face honestly and openly the
women-to-women conflicts that in the past have compromised our individual and collective potential.

Current research tells us that women's sensitivity to
others and ability to manage a cooperative workplace give us
great advantage in the business world. Our strengths, however, anticipate our challenges. Conflicts deriving from
relationship demands, competition issues, and personal sensitivity have plagued us in the past. But we can break the old
patterns and offer each other—and ourselves—new freedom and
opportunities. Only by learning how to be our best together can
we create the mutual support structure we need to protect the
advances we have made and the future we have earned.

I believe that such a future is possible and am dedicated to making it happen. That's why we founded WomenWorks, Inc., a training business dedicated to positive working relationships among women. The idea for WomenWorks began over a cup of coffee in the spring of 1987. Betty Brown and I had been partners in a writing, training, and editing business since 1983. We met Barbara Cohen, a licensed psychotherapist, when we were all presenters at an out-of-town working women's conference. We discovered our offices were only blocks apart and decided, once back home, to meet and get better acquainted.

Before our second cappucino, we had discovered a mutual interest in women working with women. In her therapy practice, Barbara has helped many women resolve work-related conflicts with other women. A presentation Betty and I were asked to develop on women in partnership had led us to look at our own experience and ask other women to share their insights with us. The three of us had definite ideas about how women could work well together, but none of us knew one place where women could go to obtain such information. Before we left the coffee shop that morning, we had decided to pool our resources and develop a workshop designed specifically to tell women what they needed to know about working with other women.

One hundred and thirty women attended our first program in 1987. Since then we have trained over five thousand women from public corporations, government agencies, and professional organizations. Women leaving our workshops often ask for a book they could share with their co-workers, friends, and company managers. So I agreed to write the book, supported by Barbara's professional input and Betty's in-the-field experience as a preferred trainer for some of the country's largest corporations. We designed this book to prepare women at all levels and in any workplace circumstance to work positively and productively with each other.

As part of the process, we asked over five hundred women to tell us on an open-ended survey what they liked and did not like about working with other women. These women came from all levels within corporations and from a variety of small businesses, government entities, and professional environments. In addition, we interviewed in depth over one hundred women who shared stories from their experience about the difficulties and pleasures of working with women. Their stories and insights form the backbone of this book.

Some of these women agreed to let us use their names. Other women preferred that their names and places of work be changed or disguised. In all cases, however, the stories come from the experiences of real women in real workplace situations.

The results of our survey were surprisingly consistent. From bank tellers to entrepreneurs, from secretaries to CEOs, women consistently reported the same ideas—namely that our caring and sensitivity to other people and situations bring us together and describe our strengths while overpersonalizing, lack of self-confidence, and problems with competition threaten our unity and challenge job satisfaction.

Women who are ready to talk about working with women are also ready to listen. We will succeed because we can be honest in evaluating our style, its strengths and its challenges. As women who understand the issues, we can help each other achieve a comfortable balance between our relational needs as women and the demands of an objective, product-focused workplace.

OMNI magazine president Kathy Heaton has a dream for women of the future. "My dream for tomorrow's woman is not that she become like a man," Heaton says, "but that she influence the future with her own intellect, values and perceptions." Knowing ourselves, we can create our future. Together we can redefine what it means for women to work with women. Becoming our best together is a responsibility women share. This book is our contribution.

Women's Four Comfort Zones

1

Finding Your Comfort Zones

Denise, a successful businesswoman in her mid-forties, arrived at the office before 8:00 to prepare for a 9:00 staff meeting she had called. At 8:45 she checked her makeup and applied a light brushing of lipstick. The clock said 8:50 as she scanned her notes for the last time, keeping herself busy until just before she could leave her office and arrive in the conference room at exactly 9:00. That way she could avoid the chit-chat about home buying or after-school child care that inevitably arose when the women on her project had a few minutes free. When she arrived, everyone instantly stopped talking and Denise took her seat.

Denise had been in her new position for two months, overseeing a team of writers who produced publications for business and industry contracts. She opened her meeting with a list of comments addressed to different members of the group. "Althea, this doesn't work for the overall approach I outlined last week. Go back to the memo I distributed on style and revise according to my notes. Marian, your article needs more background. When you work on your own, you're responsible for the full scope. I thought you had learned from your experience on the institute feature. Julie, I'll take over the corporation history section. Just leave me your notes. You can then concentrate on corporate gifts and community projects. You're struggling, Julie, and we have a deadline."

Denise then distributed a memo outlining the final timetable for the project. Promptly at 9:30 she reinforced the importance of getting revised sections to her for approval, snapped her briefcase shut, and left the room.

Later that day, Denise declined an invitation to celebrate Althea's birthday at a nearby restaurant, claiming she wanted to maintain her concentration on the new project. When a former secretary stopped by in the afternoon with her four-week-old son, Denise closed her door and scowled her disapproval to the group for gathering to admire the baby. At the end of the day, she took the stairs to avoid the cluster of women exchanging small talk at the elevator.

As the project progressed, Denise continued the meetings which served more to coordinate her timetable than to update the group on how the project was coming together. Denise had a clear sense of the overall concept, but she did not feel it necessary to share her vision or ask for input. When she met with her staff individually, she held their work up to her high standards and used the sessions to criticize weaknesses and reinforce the need for quality production. She felt in control of the project and couldn't afford to be distracted if she were to meet her deadlines.

Six weeks after that morning meeting, Ann, the chief editor, called Denise into her office. Through the glass walls the other women watched as Ann, an experienced and popular manager, leaned forward and addressed Denise directly. The stacks of copy Denise had brought went unnoticed as

Ann spoke earnestly. When some thirty minutes later Ann finished talking, Denise did not respond. For a few minutes she sat straight back in her seat. Then slowly she collected her papers, stacking them neatly before she rose to leave the office. Tears had left dark smudges of mascara on her cheeks. No one spoke as Denise walked past the other women to her office down the hall.

Ann had not talked with Denise about the project or about her performance as an editor. What she had discussed concerned Denise's management style. The other women on Denise's team had complained that they "just couldn't work with that woman." Denise's imperious, distant style had alienated the women on her publication team. As a result, productivity had declined and morale was uncharacteristically low. Ann decided she had to intervene before losing some promising young writers or having to let a talented and experienced project leader go.

Denise had majored in English and journalism in college before shifting to marketing as a graduate student. She got her first job in 1973 as marketing director for an engineering company where she and the secretary/receptionist were the only women among twenty-seven men. Denise, like other women in the seventies, studied books on the corporate system and played the game well. She plotted her moves, with respect to office politics, and collected rewards for bottom-line performance. But when she began her new job with Ann's company, she encountered a team of women, and she wasn't prepared for the differences between the men she had learned to work with and the women who made up her current team.

Ann recognized Denise's situation and offered to help. She began by suggesting that the younger women Denise encountered on her new team were not accustomed to this "masculine" style from a woman and rebelled against it.

How Far We've Come

Denise's difficulties reflect a dramatic change in the workplace that has evolved slowly over the past two decades. Twenty-five years ago, when women began entering the work force in waves, many of us believed we had to be just like men to prove we were just as good as men. We studied books on male leadership style and tried to leave our feminine traits outside the corporate doors. We practiced assertiveness, refused to be distracted from the bottom line, played a male game of organizational politics (when we had the chips), and let everyone know nothing would distract us from our career goals.

And we did well! Though a "glass ceiling" still exists for highly trained and talented women, we have proven that we lack nothing in the way of talent, skill, and determination. Since 1983, for example, the number of female managers has increased from 3.5 million to 6.1 million. By 1992, according to *Megatrends for Women*, women-owned businesses will employ more people than the Fortune 500!

Felice Schwartz, founder of Catalyst, an organization dedicated to women's advancement in the workplace, has been studying women for thirty years. In her 1992 book *Breaking With Tradition*, she states with conviction that women have proven without a doubt we are "just as good" as men. Schwartz's "cardinal sin," the sin that ignited the "Mommy Track" debate in the late eighties, was to suggest that women are not the same as men. Schwartz argues it is vital for the future of business that we recognize and respect the distinction: women are just as good, but not the same, as men. For both men and women, honoring that difference is crucial for successful relationships at work.

In the past, many of us women have found ourselves caught in the conundrum created when our differences are not honored. If we acted like men, men often felt threatened by our directness and competitiveness, and many women found us alienating and difficult to work with. On the other hand, if we acted like women—seeming reluctant to play power politics and insisting on bringing relationship-based values into an objective, competitive "male" workplace—men found our "feminine" behaviors a sign of weakness, and women who emulated the male style felt uncomfortable. In a sense, we were damned whatever we did. We weren't sure who we should be, and other women weren't sure what they wanted us—or themselves—to be either.

Today the scene is changing. As we have proved our competence, our confidence has grown. We see more women in the upper levels of our corporations and professions. We no longer feel we must act like men to have a chance at success. Researchers, among them Sally Helgesen and Judy B. Rosener, have identified what they call a female work style. This style not only has been successful for managerial women, but offers a new model for corporations in the future.

Women who represent the female style value personal relationships with their co-workers and staff. Power and influence for these women relies on a "web" of connections, rather than position on a hierarchical ladder. They demonstrate caring and motivate others by encouraging and recognizing personal growth. They value cooperation over competition and invite others to share information and power rather than protect status for themselves.

Only recently have there been significant numbers of women at noticeably high levels in business and industry modeling an effective female style. An older generation of women didn't have this model. As a result, conflicts sometimes exist between older and younger women over expectations for workplace behaviors.

Trudi Ferguson, president of a southern California management firm that deals with women in organizations, studied fifty successful women in law, medicine, the arts, business, and entertainment. She observed that the older women she studied had adopted masculine models and attributed their success primarily to ability, competence, and independence. Younger women, by contrast, cited getting along with people and being sensitive and understanding as explanations for their success. These younger women, more confident of their place in the work world, were comfortable expressing feminine values at work and expected other women to exhibit these values also. As the authors of *Megatrends for Women* note, "Most women never learned the military style of management and would have been laughed out of the office if they did. There was really no alternative but for women to create their own way. It was completely in tune with the megatrends of the day and is now the dominant leadership model."

Denise, however, studied and adopted the masculine style. Being detached, self-sufficient, and productivity-focused had been effective when she worked with men. Now, however, she had to learn how to balance her masculine strengths with the expectations of the women on her team who were more comfortable with a more relational and inclusive female style.

Adjusting her style definitely could improve Denise's effectiveness. According to Judy Rosener, in her summary of research conducted for the International Women's Forum, "Though most men and women describe themselves as having mixed feminine and masculine traits, women who do describe themselves as predominantly 'feminine' or 'gender-neutral' report a higher level of followership among their female subordinates than do women who describe themselves as 'masculine.'" The women on Denise's team certainly saw her style as masculine and resisted her leadership because they couldn't relate to her.

Of course, neither Denise nor any woman should adopt a style that is not her own just because it suddenly has popular acclaim. We are individuals, and as individuals express different personalities, skills, and abilities.

But we need to be aware that as we bring our style to work, we bring with it expectations for ourselves and each other that we learned as little girls growing up in a female culture. "When I say 'women in business are different from men,'" Felice Schwartz writes, "I'm really talking about a complex interplay of biology, socialization, tradition, and perception." This complex interplay of multiple factors gives us the values we express in our female work style—and creates the difficulties women report in working together.

Conflicts arise because women have behavioral expectations for other women we do not have for men. Simply put, we make allowances for men being different from us, but when women are different, it makes us uncomfortable. Researchers Candice West and Don Zimmerman use the phrase "doing gender" to explain what happens when women or men adjust their behavior to meet the expectations of the gender with whom they are interacting. In *The Mismeasure of Women*, Carol Tavris summarizes their conclusions: "'Doing gender' represents a 'kind of silent accommodation' that we demonstrate when we interact with one gender or the other. We 'do gender' unconsciously, adjusting our behavior and our perceptions depending on the gender of the person we are working, playing, or chatting with."

At work, when we interact with men, we adjust our behavior and perceptions to meet the expectations of the male context. That's because, in a certain sense, unconsciously we don't expect men to behave as we do and so we make all kinds of accommodations to deal with the differences between us.

But when a woman doesn't behave as we expect she should, we become uneasy and may try to force the expected behavior or punish the woman for her refusal to conform. Additionally, when our expectations for women-to-women relationships clash with workplace demands, we may act inappropriately in our attempts to have our expectations met.

"Whether women are twenty, thirty, or fifty years old, whether they have a high school education or an MBA," Barbara Cohen explains, "they tend to hold certain expectations in common when working with other women. Regardless of how we ourselves may reflect these feminine values, secretly we expect other women to conform. When they don't, we can feel confused and betrayed. Listening to hundreds of women since beginning my practice in 1978, I can tell you that having at least some of those expectations met makes a positive difference in job satisfaction and performance for the women I see."

What are these expectations and where do they come from? Very generally, the feminine style includes putting great value on relationships, preferring consensus and cooperation to conflict and competition, exhibiting caring, and encouraging the growth and development of others. When Denise emphasized product over people and seemed distant and critical rather than supportive or caring, she violated her team's sense of how women should behave towards one another. And had Ann not intervened, Denise might have permanently lost the good will, and the good work, of her team.

What Are Your Comfort Zones?

We call these expectations of how women should behave at work our "comfort zones." Comfort zones are categories that describe what we tend to appreciate in a workplace environment. In order to work effectively with other women, it's very important for you to know what your comfort zones are and how they compare with those of other women. Clashes in comfort zones make up a significant portion of women-to-women work conflicts. So please take a minute to consider the statements on the following inventory. Keep track of how often you agree, disagree, or are neutral on each statement.

COMFORT ZONE INVENTORY	agree	neither agree nor disagree	disagree
1. I see my company, or work group, as my family.			
2. I believe taking time during the day for non-job-related conversations helps create a positive climate and develops friendliness among women.			
3. I believe I have a responsibility to support my company, even when I see problems that may threaten my job.			
4. I believe that maintaining good relationships with co-workers works better than using power and authority to encourage performance.			
5. I like co-workers and managers to comment/ask about my personal life and events outside of work.			
6. I feel comfortable accepting or giving a hug to acknowledge support or understanding.			
7. I am most comfortable when I feel my co-workers are my friends.			
8. It is important to me that people at work acknowledge and support my self-worth.			
9. I take time to understand all the dimensions of a problem before I act.			
10. I believe my training and skills should assure me recognition and reward.			
11. I want to be fully prepared before pursuing a promotion or volunteering for a new assignment.			
12. I believe it makes good sense to spend time gathering input from many people before I make a final decision.			
13. I believe organizations that stress status and power pit people against each other and create a disruptive environment.			
14. I feel comfortable sharing power and information.			
15. I believe teams accomplish more if they take time to define and understand the process they will use to accomplish a goal.			
16. I feel more comfortable cooperating than I do competing.			
TOTAL CHECKS:			

If you agree with the statements more often than you disagree or remain neutral, your choices coincide with those of the 513 women who answered our survey. These women told us that they appreciate the understanding that can exist among women. They value the fact that women can talk about themselves with other women and "share their feelings." They like that women can offer friendship and caring, that women support one another and "take time to listen." They appreciate female co-workers who "go the extra mile," "work hard," and "know their stuff." These women also like women who "cooperate," "share," "help," and work well as "team players."

We have taken what these women tell us they appreciate about women in a positive working environment and divided their responses into four comfort zones. If you look back at the inventory, you can see how your preferences fit into these categories. Numbers 1-4 refer to valuing relationship or *connecting* with people at work. The next four, 5-8, refer to personal involvement or *caring*. Items 9-12 concern *being competent* and the importance we put on doing a good job and making sound decisions. The final four, 13-16, relate to a preference for *cooperating and sharing* over competition and power tactics.

In our workshops, comfort zones serve as a convenient model to talk about the elements of female style and what can cause difficulties among women. These comfort zones may not be mutually exclusive and certainly follow no scientific principle, but they do help us talk about issues that affect women-to-women workplace relationships.

In short, problems result at work when we disregard the comfort zones many women find essential to job satisfaction and performance. As our survey results suggest, women who value connecting with other women dislike being cut out of a relationship network and are especially upset if they perceive a relationship results in betrayal. An uncaring woman who doesn't attend to the self-esteem needs of her co-workers or subordinates can create a very negative workplace environment. So can women who refuse to recognize the competence of other women or take responsibility for their own value. Women who prefer a cooperative setting where people share information and support, feel uncomfortable in competitive situations where each woman seems to be out for herself.

Balance Is the Key

In a nutshell, respecting these comfort zones leads to successful relationships with other women. Denise, for one, could benefit from acknowledging these comfort zones. She could take a few minutes before a meeting to get to know the women on her team and to let them know her. Instead of being so direct and critical, she could demonstrate caring by recognizing accomplishment and making suggestions for personal growth. She could let the women know she respects their competence by asking for their ideas and sharing her own. This way Denise could build a cooperative community, a team, rather than reign as a powerful director.

However, most of us are not like Denise. The greatest challenge for many of us who already feel comfortable with our feminine style comes not from how to "be more like a woman," but from how to balance our comfort zone needs with the demands of the workplace.

Caring, out of control, puts too much emphasis on the personal and can draw attention away from more pertinent workplace issues. An overemphasis on our connection with individuals and cliques can also seriously inhibit opportunities to move into new situations. And when we do move to new groups or receive promotions, connection issues can threaten the support we need from other women to succeed in our new positions. Caretaking also, if not monitored, can deny over-protected women the experiences they need to develop their own strengths and skills. And the personal obligation that follows some forms of caring can set women up for betrayal when relationship expectations conflict with work priorities.

When we abuse the competence comfort zone, we may let our need to feel fully prepared keep us from risking new responsibilities. Or when women exhibit extraordinary competence, they sometimes threaten other women who see the competent ones as asserting their superiority and setting themselves apart.

Finally, when we insist on cooperation as the only model for working together, we make it difficult for women to compete openly and confidently for opportunities that will advance their own careers and enhance the position of all women.

Thus, abusing the comfort zones by taking them to extremes creates as many problems for women as ignoring them altogether. The solution to positive women-working-with-women relationships lies in balance: not too much and not too little.

We can achieve such a balance within ourselves and we must maintain a balance between what other women expect from us and our responsibilities to our jobs. We can do this by first developing an understanding of where we stand vis-à-vis each comfort zone, and then by honestly looking at what might happen if we let our comfort zone needs dominate workplace responsibilities. Finally, in accepting our responsibility to one another, we can act to eliminate our problems and realize together the opportunities our feminine style offers for a powerful future.

2

Needing to Connect

Women define themselves primarily through relationship to others. Indeed, as Anne Wilson Schaef writes in *Women's Reality*, "In the female system, the center of the universe is relationship." That's why in our survey, a vast majority of women cited that "good relationships" at work contribute significantly to their job satisfaction. Many other studies that ask women what factors are important in determining their job satisfaction repeatedly cite "relationships with co-workers" as one of the top five factors. (In contrast, relationships seldom appear in the top ten factors for men. Factors both men and women list include salary, benefits, challenge, and "a chance to get ahead.") This truth has enormous significance for how women work together, but it's only in the last ten years or so that we have begun to understand the implications.

Part of the groundbreaking work on the topic was done by Carol Gilligan in her important study of female moral development, *In a Different Voice*. She contrasts masculine gender identity, which is based on separation, with female identity, which is defined by attachment and threatened by separation. She cites the research of Lawrence Kohlber and Janet Lever who both observed that when children play games, girls are likely to end the game when quarrels arise rather than risk damaging or losing a relationship. "Girls subordinated the continuation of the game to the continuation of the relationships," Gilligan writes, "in contrast to the boys who relied on elaborating a system of rules to handle their disputes." Gilligan goes on to observe that women give primary consideration to "a network of connection, a web of relationships that is sustained by a process of communication."

The network image has become an important element in understanding the female work style for the '90s. Sally Helgesen, in her study of four successful female business leaders, *The Female Advantage: Women's Ways of Leadership*, notes that the women she studied structured their organizations more like networks of connecting relationships than hierarchies which placed people above or below each other on a ladder of power. Like the women we surveyed, these women valued their close personal connections with the other women, and men, on their teams.

Katherine McLeod, professor emeritus in social work and currently a clinical social worker in private practice, understood women's need for relationship long before the current wave of research hit the stands. "Women," she states from experience, "always pursue relationship. Relationship comes first. Task is supplemented by the need for relationship. When connecting doesn't happen, task suffers."

Two-thirds of the women in our survey spontaneously listed positive factors related to the connection and mutual understanding women can experience together. They told us they liked that women can "empathize," "relate," "identify with each other." They told us that they feel comfortable when women "talk," "communicate," "share feelings as well as facts," "bring the personal into the job." What women told us they didn't like focused on co-workers and bosses who appeared "cold," "distant," or "superior." In essence, they weren't comfortable with women who didn't let them connect.

Talk to Me

As our survey results imply, what connects women is conversation. "Women," writes Robin Tolmach Lakoff in *Talking Power: The Politics of Language*, "need to be in constant communication in order to . . . preserve feeling(s) of trust." We talk to share personal information about ourselves that we believe other women will relate to and "understand." We talk as a way to bridge our separateness. We talk to find out how we are alike.

"For most women," notes Deborah Tannen in *You Just Don't Understand: Men and Women in Conversation*, "the language of conversation is primarily a language of rapport: a way of establishing connections and negotiating relationships." In contrast, "for most men talk is primarily a means to preserve independence and negotiate and maintain status in a hierarchical social order." Therefore, men are more apt to use language to establish who does what, who can challenge whom, who has status or power.

Rather than establishing a pecking order, talk among women creates bonds and holds them together. In conversation, we look for common ground. Talk can, of course, be about work and serve to support the communication needed to build and maintain a cooperative, connected environment. But it can also be, and often is, about our personal lives—our families, our feelings, our "humanism."

By talking to one another about "personal" issues at work, we are carrying out an essential function that will often make us a more cohesive team or work group. I know, for example, of a group of university nutritionists who intentionally allow five minutes before their weekly meetings just to "catch up" on each other's lives. They share whose children are doing what, who has found a wonderful massage therapist, even how a divorce settlement is progressing. This personal talk helps connect the group and establishes a comfortable base for the work they do together.

Wherever we come together, women use talk to establish connection. I observed women using language this way at a recent conference lunch. I was seated at a table of eight, and after one hour I knew who in the group had children, who liked her job, who wished she had more time to study botanical drawing, and who had been disappointed with her birthday celebration. Of course, we also discussed the future of training and the impact of interactive video on instruction. But the shared talk about our personal lives brought us together and made us "real" to each other.

My husband, Bill, on the other hand, can return from a week of solar energy task force meetings and not know if his colleagues have families, let alone if they find their lives fulfilling. He will know who is doing what task, where people have been hang gliding, how the fishing was in Italy. In other words, he will know the activities that make up his colleagues' lives, but not the feelings that for most women make life real.

When Women Don't Connect

Our survey results, along with the research done elsewhere, certainly suggest that women who are willing to connect have a better chance of establishing positive relationships with other women than those who choose a more detached style. When Denise, the leader on the corporate publications project, avoided talking with the other women on her staff, she denied them a way to connect with her. As a result, they felt dissatisfied and their productivity suffered.

The situation might have evolved differently had Denise taken another tack. The fact is, she had opportunities to connect, but refused. She wouldn't participate in chitchat before meetings because she believed it wasted time. She didn't join the other women in admiring the new baby for five minutes because it interrupted her busy schedule, and because she believed the workplace should never be tainted with the sentiments of domestic life. She felt uncomfortable in participating in birthday and other get-togethers where the conversation would center on other women's personal lives. For Denise, a personal life had no relevance to the job. All that mattered was how well she performed the tasks assigned.

In addition, Denise's position of authority may have created barriers for the other women who wanted to find a base for connecting with her. Denise's style invited criticism, not of her competence, but of her ability to measure up as a woman. Women can comfortably connect with other women, including powerful women in leadership and management positions, if they can relate to her "female" qualities.

As feminist therapist Katherine McLeod explains, "When women are confronted with a new female boss, they respond first by assessing her willingness to connect, to reveal who she is, how she measures up as a woman." If they decide they can relate to her as a woman, they will offer their support and she's off to a great start. If they can't connect, they may resist her authority and their performance will suffer until they find a place on the personal level where they can relate and connect.

We assess another woman's femininity by looking for

signs of emotional responsiveness. We want to be reassured that she, like us, can be affected by the behaviors and feelings of others. In Denise's situation, that point of relating came when the other women saw Denise respond to Ann's criticism with tears—quickly controlled, but tears nonetheless. The women on the team could relate to Denise's reaction. Suddenly she became real to them. Crying is something women do; by crying, Denise revealed she was one of us. The women on her publication team could then connect with her femaleness, and their ability to identify with another person showed these women that behind the controlled facade Denise, too, was vulnerable.

While it took more than watching Denise leave Ann's office with smudged mascara for the women on her team to feel completely comfortable, having a point of connection made Denise seem more "real" as a woman. When she did later try to establish a more personal rapport, the other women already had a base for connection.

Avoiding the Rumor Mill

Along with resistance and attacks on their femaleness, women who don't easily connect with other women often have to confront rumors. By not making themselves available to other women, by not letting themselves be known, they leave themselves vulnerable to speculation. That's because our need to know something of the personal life of another woman, to make her seem real, compels us to invent a history to fill the void she leaves open.

To fill in what they didn't know about Denise, the women on her staff had begun speculating about why she had left her previous job. Speculation became rumors—and rumors, when repeated often enough, begin to sound like true stories. By the time Ann realized how serious the problems between Denise and her group had become, rumors were rampant: Denise had been fired because she alienated clients with her domineering style; she had taken credit for work her subordinates did and they went to management to complain; she lost a major account when her affair with the client ended. One rumor said she had even given up custody of her daughter so she could devote full attention to her career! Fortunately, Denise had a sensitive manager who encouraged her to become more open with her team. With Ann's encouragement, Denise learned how to modify her behaviors so that she could replace rumor with fact while still maintaining the privacy she valued.

Denise became more open at work and began connecting with the writers on her all-female team. She relaxed her strict injunction against chitchat and arrived outside the conference room five minutes before the scheduled meeting. Though she didn't feel comfortable sharing intimacies, she entered the conversations with comments on new restaurants or references to books she had read. In this way, she was able to talk with the other women about her personal life without feeling uncomfortable or compromising herself.

At first awkwardly, then with genuine interest in the rich lives of the women on her staff, Denise joined the group for celebration lunches or an occasional Friday after hours. When she landed a contract for a large corporation's annual report, Denise called a congratulatory lunch herself, and everyone on the staff attended. As relationships developed, it became easier for Denise to communicate her criticisms and suggestions because she knew more about the personalities of her team and what motivated them to do well. Because they were growing to like Denise, her staff cared about meeting her high expectations. They felt connected to her and she could rely on her personal power, rather than organizational position or authority, to encourage productivity and receive support.

Women like Denise, who choose independence rather than connection and involvement with other women, frequently find themselves the objects of hostility. Patty, a research assistant who is naturally self-contained and somewhat shy, believed not getting involved with the other women in her lab would protect her from gossip and "other problems." To avoid her female co-workers, she went home every day at lunch and left the lab exactly at 5. She rejected offers to join the group for their Friday pizza lunches and she *never* volunteered information about her after-work activities.

In her absence, rumors flourished. One was that Patty had failed her Ph.D. qualifying exam and was spending every spare minute preparing to sue her major professor, one of the engineers whose research the women all supported. Patty's independence and distance irritated the other women who took her as "snobby" and "superior acting." The name they used for her, "Rat Tail," in reference to her long blond braid, had caught on even among the graduate students. At lab review sessions and on project reports, her co-workers didn't mention her contributions or minimized her efforts even though she was a good and conscientious worker.

We met Patty and a co-worker, Marla, at one of our seminars. Marla had recognized a problem with Patty's unwillingness to connect and had insisted Patty attend our workshop. Marla hoped for some ideas that would ease the tension in the lab. We talked with both women at a break, explaining that Patty's reluctance to get involved with the women she worked with violated the connection comfort zone of her co-workers. Barbara suggested Patty make a gesture toward meeting her co-workers halfway. That didn't mean Patty had to go for pizza every Friday, but that she might consider joining the group at least once a month. She also suggested Patty try listening to and commenting on what the other women had to say about their lives. When the time seemed right, Patty might also say something about her own activities and interests.

Barbara saw Patty five months later. Patty had taken the pizza lunch suggestion, and one day the conversation turned to dogs. Patty, it turns out, had plenty to say about breeds and personalities. The other women were fascinated when they learned Patty trained Dobermans as watchdogs. When she mentioned having to get home to let her dogs run, the women finally understood why she left at lunch and right after work. Since then, occasionally someone would mention something about dogs, and Patty would comfortably enter the conversation. Tensions had relaxed and with it the efforts to punish Patty for her "absence" and detachment.

Like Patty, not all women want to spend work time or their precious after-work hours connecting with other women. Yet many of the same women recognize that connecting creates a friendly environment that supports good working relationships with other women, and they make the effort.

Anna, an elementary school teacher, doesn't get excited about most of the social activities women plan to soften the hard edges of their teaching jobs. She feels connected to the other teachers through their mutual dedication to the students. However, she does see that getting together after work to celebrate a birthday or anniversary helps unite the staff on a personal level. She believes ultimately the students benefit from good relations among the teachers, and that matters to her. "I can't see doing the organizing for these get-togethers myself," she concedes, "but I appreciate the women who take the time to bring us together. It definitely has value."

Forging Connections

If you're in a work situation where you don't feel sufficient connection, you can do something to change the situation. Sandy is a former teacher who had gone to work for the marketing department of a large computer company. She found herself one day in 1987 doing well in her new career, but dissatisfied and tired from "playing a role that didn't feel quite right." The organization reflected a male emphasis on position, power, and product, and had little tolerance for personal connection. The women with whom she worked were all well-educated, well-paid, and appreciated for their ability to produce top-notch work. They represented a confident group of engineers, technical writers, and project managers who kept their workplace exchanges focused on marketing issues. The approach worked on the surface, but the sense of detachment wasn't conducive to making the workplace a comfortable environment for these women. They wanted to know each other, to have a way of connecting beyond, or deeper than, who contributed what to a new product promotion.

So one day, Sandy posted an invitation for an after-work dinner at a local restaurant. The first evening, eight women came. They talked about their non-work-related lives and became, as Sandy said, "real to each other." Knowing who else had a junior high school daughter with bizarre tastes in clothes, or that the woman with the engineering degree was once a drama major and had played Ophelia in a summer Shakespearean production allowed the women to connect. When, on Monday morning, Sandy could ask Joan how her kayaking weekend had been, or stop by Jenelle's desk and inquire how her mother was doing after surgery, their comfort level on the job increased. They maintained a high-level commitment to the job; but what became their monthly dinner out changed their relationship to each other and to their job satisfaction. Most probably it increased their productivity as well. To honor their efforts, they christened their group MWOM, Mature Women of Marketing. The group continued to meet as some women moved away, new women joined, and promotions affected their workday interactions.

Interestingly, this female response to a male work environment provides an example of how women can take charge of having their needs met at work. In this case, the women played their roles in the traditional male structure but compensated by establishing a parallel work community based on personal talk to create connection. A similar group at Levi Strauss has formed to serve a comparable purpose. If you find yourself frustrated in a very rigid "male" work environment, you might want to try forming a female work community with your co-workers.

The Gossip Challenge

Connecting with women at work forms the base for positive working relationships. However, taken to the extreme, the need to connect can become one of the most destructive factors for women who work with women.

Personal talk, what we often refer to as "gossip," can be extremely divisive in a work setting. It' s a natural tendency, though. "For most women . . . intimacy rests on talk—both 'deep talk' about significant feelings and worries and 'small talk' about daily events," writes Carol Tavris in *The Mismeasure of Women*. "Women like to talk about personal matters such as their feelings and relationships; they are willing, often eager, to reveal weaknesses and fears."

And with whom do we talk this way? We talk to women because women listen. We sympathize and validate one another's experiences by relating them to their own lives. We offer comfort in times of need and seek solace in our difficulties. What we don't always remember, however, is that anything we say can also be used against us. Women who use talk to build trust are not always trustworthy when it comes to how they use what they hear.

The problem is exacerbated by the realities of our lives. Today many of us have little time for talk with women outside work. The women we spend most of our time with, who are there when we are upset or excited, are the women we spend eight hours, even twelve hours, a day working alongside. But when another woman uses what we reveal in a way that hurts us, either in our absence or to embarrass us with others, the talk that had good intentions turns sour. The personal talk we share can be seriously disruptive when a woman uses shared intimacies to embarrass a co-worker or "even the score." Gossip becomes negative when we switch from "talking about" to "talking against," according to Deborah Tannen.

Using gossip in this way is very tempting to women because we've been socialized to not be direct and confrontational. In *Opposite Sides of the Bed: A Lively Guide to the Differences Between Women and Men*, Cris Evatt cites research conducted by a University of Denver psychologist, Donald Sharpsteen, on the gossip patterns of three hundred fifty men and women. Sharpsteen observes that "retribution is a powerful motive for women's gossip. Rather than expressing anger directly, women gossip about someone they are mad at." Thus the intimate talk that connects us can become fodder for an attack when our confidant becomes irritated or angry.

When, for example, an architect named Sibyl confided in her co-worker Joyce that she was upset by her former husband's conviction on an illegal gambling charge, Sybil set herself up for Joyce's vindictive gossip. The situation that gave Joyce her opportunity happened when Sibyl accused Joyce of delaying a design proposal because her estimates were taking too long. Joyce was angry that Sibyl didn't understand the extra time design changes had required on the estimates. Rather than confronting Sibyl directly about her accusation, Joyce retaliated by telling everyone that Sibyl's ex-husband was in jail and that Sybil seemed "inappropriately upset." The information had nothing to do with work, but it served to make Sibyl uncomfortable and, for a while at least, affected her position as leader of the design group.

Gossip hurts most, though, when women intentionally use shared intimacies to destroy an enemy or a competitor. Marie violated Yvonne's trust when she publicized Yvonne's future dreams to undermine Yvonne's bid for a promotion at the scientific instruments company where they both worked. Yvonne had told Marie that she wanted someday to live in Idaho and start up a water testing service for small environmentally-conscious companies. She shared also that she was unhappy with her domestic situation but was trying to work things out. When the company's growth created the need for a new marketing manager, both Yvonne and Marie applied. Marie, however, felt it "her responsibility to the company" to let upper management know about Yvonne's "lack of commitment" and "unstable marriage." Though Yvonne assured the team who interviewed her that she wanted the job very much and that her plans for Idaho were "only a dream for the distant future," they believed they couldn't afford to risk having her learn the new position and then leave them after a year or two. Marie got the job.

It is hard for us to monitor our talk with other women. We want to be honest, to share our feelings and experiences, but we need to stay aware of what might hurt us if a friendly situation turns nasty. We can protect ourselves and control opportunities for other women to use our personal stories negatively if we limit our intimacies to good experiences and neutral events in our lives. Women have a tendency to seek solace for our fears, failures, and weaknesses; however, we should seek some shoulder to cry on that is outside the workplace.

Constantly watching what we say can be exhausting. Protecting our image rather than being ourselves feels wrong to many of us who appreciate trust and connection with others. However, we must be aware that not everyone will treat our disclosures in the way we intend them to be used. The fewer opportunities we allow for the misuse of personal talk, the better we will protect ourselves and the women we work with from destructive consequences.

I want to end this discussion of personal talk with one more warning: be especially careful how you use personal disclosure in hostile situations. The good intentions of using talk to establish friendliness can backfire and fuel the feud rather than cure the problem.

Too Much of a Good Thing

Personal talk properly monitored can establish connection among women, but once women have connected, can relationship binds get out of control?

Do you remember cliques? They haunted us in eighth grade and mined the fields of high school. When cliques form, an exaggerated sense of commitment to a group can hold us back from moving on to new and better opportunities.

Clique. The word makes women shudder. Its pejorative connotation carries images of exclusion, narrowness, and collective meanness. Cliques are a challenge to positive women working with women relationships.

I was surprised that on our survey only thirty of over

five hundred women mentioned "cliques" by name as problems for women who work together. Maybe we've become conscious of the dangers cliques present. Maybe we are refusing to form cliques. Maybe the women who answered our surveys were on the inside enjoying the "support" and connection of a clique rather than on the outside looking in.

But, in contrast to the women answering the survey, the women we interviewed suggest that cliques remain a problem at work. They may use other words, such as "in groups," "the us-es and the thems," but words don't disguise the problem. Cliques are socially exclusive groups within a larger group or organization. Their emphasis on sameness and homeostasis, justifies (to them) their exclusion of women who just "don't fit the mold."

Cliques form because women want to feel connected. "A clique," Barbara explains, "represents the extreme in connection." Within a clique, members feel included and exclusive. But cliques can do tremendous damage.

Fran's confrontations with a clique at work have detracted from the accomplishments and recognitions that should have made her feel successful and proud. The clique consists of intensely career-committed women who do marketing for an international medical products company. These women have come through the ranks together, though their backgrounds vary from biology and business to technical writing. They know each other well and are fiercely protective of their hard-won power and position. Fran, on the other hand, entered the division from outside, having been involved as a consultant on one of the company's co-products. She contributed her talents to the team and so impressed upper management with her abilities and performance that they hired her.

Fran concedes that her manner might be considered aggressive and her style direct, but she believed all of the women involved are professionals who put the job first. She assumed they would respect her choice to do whatever it takes to produce the highest quality results.

On the surface, the marketing group functions, she tells me, but the cliquishness of the other women has made working with them a "miserable, unhappy, unhealthy experience. They exclude me in every way possible," she says. "They share information among themselves that puts me at a disadvantage during meetings when I don't know what's going on. They act politely, but they group together to criticize my ideas even though they often end up adopting my proposals as their own.

"I have tried everything to make friends and be included," she tells me. "I offer to lend my car in an emergency. I have even brought in one of my suits so one of the women could wear it for a presentation in Boston. I publicly compliment them. Nothing works. They won't let me in."

At this point, Fran, with her advanced degrees and her well-paying job, has to fight back tears. "The thing is," she says, "they just don't like me. I'm both horrified that it matters, and I hurt because it does. I recently asked three of these women, one after the other, to please pick up product samples for me while I was out of town and leave them on my desk. Not an imposition in any way. Each of these women gave me an excuse and refused. I don't know what to do and, frankly, I am considering quitting."

Fran still hasn't resolved her problems at work. She is serious about returning to consulting or perhaps teaching at a university where "I won't have to deal with cliques and can choose to spend time with people who like me." If she does, her company will lose a talented woman. Eventually, women within the clique will want to move on and the dynamics of the group will change. Until then, however, chances are the women in the clique will gain a reputation within their company for their exclusivity and cliquishness. Other women moving up in their organization may get wind of the clique's reputation and offer their abilities elsewhere.

Cliquish behavior doesn't help women, and it can exclude and destroy us. We can't allow cliques to eliminate from positions of influence, indeed from any position, women whose talents and commitments are leading them to the top.

Cliques such as the one Fran faced can make joining a new group or team difficult and demoralizing. Look now at what can happen if a clique draws together to reject a new supervisor or manager because she appears as an "outsider."

Audrey was a nurse at a large New England hospital. Intelligent, competent, and with a natural ability to comprehend organizational structure and management practice, she found herself at a major decision point: to continue as a staff nurse or make a move into management. She had recently joined a staff of operating room nurses who had been experiencing dissatisfaction with how decisions were being made and procedures redefined. The group wasn't working well as a team, and the hospital administration realized a change was needed to bring the department back to optimum function. This group of nurses had been together over five years and, though complaining about their supervisor's style and decision-making abilities, took no initiative to change the situation internally. Together they had complained to administration about Ellen, their supervisor, becoming too directive. As a group, they presented a united front.

Audrey knew how tight this group had become. When she was offered the job of replacing Ellen as supervisor, she agonized over her decision. Even though the nurses had complained about Ellen, Ellen had still been one of them. They would not welcome an outsider in their territory. Audrey's sensitivity to women's connections almost made her say no. But she wanted more challenge and eventually accepted the job, even though she knew "everyone will hate me if I do this."

Audrey's assessment of the situation had been right on target. The other nurses believed that she had taken Ellen's job away. In their reaction, they saw Audrey as a challenge to their group, their way of doing things, and their closed society. Also, Audrey believes, they felt guilty about having brought their complaints to the administration's attention. They didn't like the possibility that they had betrayed one of their own.

Audrey had to confront not only the challenge of a management position, but also the hostility of a group of women who made no secret of resenting her presence, who greeted her with insubordination just one step from mutiny. They sabotaged her meetings by coming late and leaving early. They refused to go to lunch and get to know Audrey on a more casual basis. They resisted all invitations to participate in managing their department's policies and procedures.

Audrey confronted the clique persistently. She let it be known that she worked with some of the most skilled nurses at the hospital. She went to bat for her department on support staff requests. She encouraged the nurses to visit with her anytime with ideas for improving their service to patients and surgeons—or just to get better acquainted. She never criticized Ellen's management approaches, and she gave individual women praise and credit for ideas they contributed. Audrey didn't challenge the clique but treated members as individuals. She offered respect and the women grew to respect her in return. The clique relaxed its boundaries, and a new team emerged with Audrey as the accepted and appreciated leader.

Like Audrey, we can confront cliques and create a more open, inclusive workplace. And as more and more women-owned businesses start up and hire women, we should be aware of the possibilities of cliques so we can stop them before they even start. The value and comfort of connection is lost when women put up walls. We need to acknowledge connection, and we need to make it available to everyone.

The Ties That Bind

In support of connection, women will sometimes make decisions at work that emphasize maintaining a relationship over making a career move or accepting a promotion. Women recognize sameness as a basis for connection. I realize now that a good friend almost gave up a new career direction because it meant we would no longer be alike and our relationship would change.

My friend Lynn and I both taught English at a high school in Santa Clara, California. We further defined our similarity by creating an "us against them" situation with the guidance counselors who served our students. Lynn and I opposed the way the counselors seemed to respond to student complaints by changing student schedules rather than consulting with teachers and getting to the root cause of a problem. We would sit with other teachers during lunch and share horror stories about counselors who "could never make it in the classroom so they got their counseling credentials." Secretly we knew the counselors had good training and were dedicated to their work, but the "us" and "them" approach somehow reinforced our connection.

Lynn had silently been struggling with a decision to end a difficult marriage. She had to face supporting herself and planning for a secure retirement. A natural direction for her was to complete a counseling credential and then prepare for an administrative position. Though she quietly began taking courses at night, she didn't feel comfortable enough to admit she was considering becoming "one of them." She later told me that after she realized our relationship would change, she had delayed her commitment to completing her courses and leaving the classroom to join the counseling staff.

Fortunately, and properly, Lynn decided to make the necessary career move and trusted that our relationship would adjust to the change. Of course, her announcement came as a surprise. I admit to having felt hurt that she hadn't told me earlier and abandoned by her switch to the other side. She had broken our covenant of sameness! The first few months after she returned from the summer, as a counselor, were awkward for both of us. Some of the old ease was gone, but we found a new basis for a positive connection: I learned from Lynn what a counselor had to consider in working with students, and she used me to keep in touch with a teacher's perspective.

Lynn and I were two people confronted with a challenge to our connection. What happens when one woman breaks the sameness connection with her co-workers and moves ahead to supervise or manage her former group? Women beginning together in a new business, or working together in an office or laboratory, often connect around the sameness of their positions. When faced with breaking that connection, some women refuse; others move ahead, but with uncertainty; still others continue their connection with the other women, but with shifted emphasis.

In 1992, I asked a group of women attending an American Management Association satellite conference on women and leadership how many of them had refused, or hesitated to pursue, a promotion that would have placed them above the women they worked with. At least half the women raised their hands. "It just wouldn't feel right," they said. "I just didn't think I could handle it." Those who held themselves back admitted to carrying resentment that affected their relationships with their co-workers. Three women said they had looked to other companies when they were ready to move ahead rather than face becoming a boss over former co-workers. Those who did change their status reported the transition difficult. They had had to put concerted effort into reassuring their former co-workers that connection could be maintained through open communication, information sharing, seeking and giving support, and continued caring for the people involved.

Amy, a twenty-nine-year-old product manager, works with other women in parallel positions. If she were promoted, she would be boss over the women with whom she now has a friendly, connected, working relationship. Amy admitted to me that she hadn't applied for a new position because she, as she says, "can't imagine managing people who have been my equal. It would seem out of balance; it just wouldn't feel right."

Amy doesn't have the flexibility to move to another division out of state, and she likes her job too much to look for another company. Like the women at the AMA conference and others we have interviewed, Amy is reluctant to disturb the sameness which reinforces her connection with the other women in her office.

Maintaining the status quo to preserve connection is not a viable alternative for women. We must not let our affinity for sameness hold other women back, or hold ourselves back. Many women have made the transition from co-worker to manager successfully, and these women should be our models.

For example, the group of marketing women I mentioned earlier, MWOM, serves as a support base for women who both appreciate connection and have individual career goals they want to achieve. These women openly discuss their interest in promotions and ask each other for information and support that will help them move ahead. By sharing their ambitions with the group and inviting the other women to become involved in their plans, they move the base of connection from sameness to mutual interest and benefit.

When Angela, for example, was promoted to manager, the other women who had helped her with portfolio suggestions and interview information felt included in her success. Angela, in turn, continued her connection with them by asking for input on decisions and sharing information on new training opportunities, decision-making policies, and the company's future direction. She also remembered her former product team members on a personal level, inquiring about children or how someone had liked her Japanese cooking class.

"When women work together," Barbara adds as a final warning about overconnecting, "potential always exists for relational issues to dominate workplace purpose. Cases when this happens most always involve women whose emotional needs are not being met at home. When a workplace has women willing to be drawn into these relational issues, it's like feeding a dark hole. The efforts to establish and maintain relationship can become all-consuming and, of course, work and productivity suffer. One reason some women become so connected at work is that not much is going on for them at home. Women need relationship or we feel lost, unanchored. When a woman has no relational context at home, she becomes even more needful of establishing connection at work."

When this dependency happens, any gesture or comment that threatens relationship requires the woman's immediate attention. She cannot get back to work until she feels comfortable. She draws others into this soap opera that becomes deeply personal and takes time away from the work purpose.

An office that conducts testing for a national high tech

company faces this situation right now. Teri attended one of our workshops "to get a clue how to break into all the relationship business and get us back to work." Her work group includes an older woman, Erma, who always has a "best friend" but seems to rotate the favor. Erma has had a falling out with her daughter and often scolds Teri, her supervisor and twenty years her junior, for not being more respectful and attentive. Erma's "best friends" get involved in Teri's education and become offended if Teri tries to put aside their comments. Everyone begins the day, according to Teri, setting up coffee break "chats" and picking a site for lunch. Who's asking and who's included takes as much effort as work. Time repairing and confirming relationships also intrudes into the afternoon hours.

Teri is responsible for maintaining quality at work. When factors are overlooked or data isn't accurate, Teri has to point this out to her group. Her "criticism" becomes part of the relationship quagmire. Teri feels she has lost control. If her group's work quality doesn't improve, her company may lose an important testing contract.

"When relationship takes precedence over task," Barbara told me when I explained the situation Teri had described, "those involved need to recognize what has happened. Then they must accept that at work, work comes first. They must be willing to look at their home situations and take responsibility for balancing their emotional needs and job demands."

Barbara advises that a trained counselor or consultant sensitive to women-with-women issues conduct this process. "Women in this situation need to redirect their emotional energies and find alternatives for relationship outside work. Most women will be willing to make this effort because, essentially, they care about their work group, and they care about their jobs."

Connecting with the Company

When I first began looking at women-working-with-women issues, I recognized early on how important good feelings between women were in establishing a positive working relationship. What I hadn't understood was that many women also connect with their workplaces as if they were bonding with a live, caring person and expect comparable caring in return. "Oh yes," Barbara instructed me, "women don't stop with people when they want to connect. They project their need to connect onto the workplace. Men are more willing to remain detached—they perceive the company as a machine where you put work in and take money or power out. Women, on the other hand, experience the company or the department they work for as a caring, almost-human creature. They connect with that creature and they expect caring and consideration in return."

Mary Catherine Bateson, daughter of Margaret Mead, notes how a woman's identification with an institution differs from a man's. Writing in her autobiographical book, *Composing a Life*, Bateson remembers how she reacted to a power struggle at Amherst College. "There was an odd mirroring between the distortions in my vision and those of a handful of senior men, equally caused by identification with the institution. I tended to identify my interests with those of the college; they identified the interests of the college with their own. The same kind of complementary distortion often happens in marriage. Women are taught to deny themselves for the sake of the marriage. Men are taught that the marriage exists to support them." As Bateson points out, women often deny themselves for the sake of the corporation, and when the corporation doesn't treat them with respect and thanks, they feel betrayed and angry.

In their fine study of why women have felt betrayed by

success, *Success and Betrayal: The Crisis of Women In Corporate America*, Sarah Hardesty and Nehama Jacobs identify a series of myths that have set women up for confusion and betrayal. One promises that the corporation will act like a family and provide safety and continuity. Women believe this even though, quoting Paula Bernstein in *Family Ties, Corporate Bond*, "The corporation cannot love us back. It makes no lifetime commitment to us the way a family does—or should." Hardesty and Jacobs go on to say, "The root of much of the eventual damage to corporate women's self-esteem comes from early, unconscious tendencies to anthropomorphize the company itself—the inanimate corporate entity—and to cast the corporation as either a proud father or a demanding lover, expecting the appropriate emotional feedback in return."

In the myth of the loyal retainer, Hardesty and Jacobs see a woman's connection to the company as an explanation for why so many women stay on in their corporations beyond a point beneficial to their careers. These women feel responsibility because of the value a company has invested in them; they feel they owe the company loyalty in return. And when they feel their loyalty to the company has been abused, they react as if to a personal betrayal—through resistance and attempts to sabotage the corporation that hurt them.

I once met a woman whose sense of connection to the company had trapped her in an almost empty office trailer on the lot of a prefabricated home business. The half-full lot and empty desks didn't suggest a thriving business. Ruth occupied the receptionist's desk. She offered me coffee and some background on the business. When asked about the market for prefabricated homes, she confided openly, "The market is not so good. We are reducing inventory and will probably close down in the next six months." I asked why she didn't leave. She answered without apology, "I can't leave. I've given them eleven good years, and they need me."

On another occasion, I encountered a group of women who had over-connected with their corporations and felt the organizations owed them something before they could detach and move on. WomenWorks had been asked to develop a program on change for a group of day care facility directors. The women in the workshop represented two companies that had recently merged, one having bought the other. The directors who had seen themselves as competitors now were working for the same corporation. Not only did they find working with their former competitors uncomfortable, they felt betrayed by the corporation to which they had given their allegiance. No one had included them in the decision to merge; no one had cared how they felt about the change.

The women with the day care organization had connected with a larger corporation. The women felt betrayed by a decision that hadn't taken their feelings into consideration. Individually and collectively, they were resisting the change and stalling the process of assimilation. They had been assured that no one would lose her job; after all, the new company had simply bought the facilities. The facilities still had to be managed, and these were the best directors available. But the women didn't see it that way. They felt as if they should have been consulted before any change took place. They complained to each other, reinforcing the belief that their former companies should have cared, but did not. They felt betrayed by the executive decision-makers and encouraged each other to resist, rather than accept, the new situation. The few women who did recognize in the new organization chances for advancement to regional positions had their optimism met with cries of "traitor."

In counseling sessions with other women in similar situations, Barbara had guided clients to see how the relationship they had assumed existed between themselves and their company could not, in reality, exist. She encouraged, for example, one woman to accept that eliminating book-keepers after a company went over to a computerized system was not a personal act against her. And once her client accepted the business reality, Barbara was able to help her develop plans for what to do next.

But trying to get this group of women to accept that an impersonal decision had been made, and that it was in their best interest to adapt to it, was more of a challenge. Together, the women held each other back from adjusting to the new structure and contributing positively to the transition.

With Barbara's guidance, they learned to accept that the corporate directors had made a bottom-line, business-based decision. Perhaps the corporate directors should have better communicated their decision, but facts are facts. The women also realized how they were sabotaging their opportunities for advancement in the new corporation by their collective resistance. They have determined to heal rather than keep their wounds open. The transition won't be easy, but it will go more smoothly now that they no longer feel personally betrayed.

For women who own companies, I can't help wondering how our desire to connect with our companies will affect our decisions to break up those companies once profits fall and the future looks grim. My partners and I have two businesses. We have invested years of our time and our selves in those businesses. Will our personal connection with these ventures distort the reality of their health and viability? I hope we will trust our good business sense and accept that, though we give of ourselves and care, our partnerships are not living, feeling entities.

We owe ourselves our best efforts. We do not owe our businesses our lives. Our companies are machines, not children. Our company, even when it is our own, does not love us. It isn't human. It doesn't ask us to sacrifice ourselves for its existence.

When It's Time to Leave

I see another challenge for women in business and for corporations who value the talented women they have attracted. As I've noted, when women form teams and work groups, connection and relationship are vital to comfort and performance. Therefore, it isn't easy for us to break those connections and walk away when a project ends or a reorganization changes our work group.

In a study by British researchers Diane McGuiness and Corinne Hutt, it was found that preschool girls spent an average of 92.5 seconds saying goodbye to their mothers at the school gate, compared to 32 seconds spent by boys. As adult working women, do we still need more time to break our connections? Men can comfortably move into new positions. Their value system depends less on relationship and more on function. They accept this and expect it of others. Women, on the other hand, need time to let go of relationships and build new ones.

As managers and directors, we must provide time and support for women during these transitions. For a Women in Technology conference, my partner, Betty, and I conducted a series of workshops on gender differences. In each session, women identified the need for corporations, especially the "male" organization for whom they worked, to provide an environment where women's strengths can thrive. One specific wish they mentioned was for more sensitivity to women's need for connection and relationship. "They can't expect us just to walk away from a team and not care," they told us. "And they need to give us opportunity to know the people we work with on the next job before we can produce 100 percent."

Building relationships takes time. Corporations need to give us that time or they may miss the advantages that relationship connection promises for tomorrow's world. Women-run businesses must also plan ahead for connection to take place. Relationship networks don't just happen. They grow from trust and our knowing and connecting with each other.

Suggestions for Healthy Work Connections

* Take time to get to know the women you work with. Plan an occasional lunch or after-work activity when you can talk comfortably and establish a personal rapport. Balance the value of knowing other women, and being known, with your own needs for privacy and professional distance.

* When you share personal stories and information, keep your exchanges positive. Respect the confidences other women share.

* Keep your work connections friendly and flexible. Don't let your need for connection overshadow your need to find the best career opportunities and situations for you. If you feel yourself stuck in a job situation that doesn't satisfy your salary or personal needs, ask yourself why you are staying. If you discover that you are reluctant to leave because the other women depend on you, or you feel obligated to them, or you would feel as if you had abandoned them if you left, reconsider your priorities. If you let connection with other women hold you back, you will model for other women that this is an acceptable way to behave in the workplace. Instead, accept that you owe it to yourself and to all women to seek the best work situation. Expect that others will understand and support your priorities.

* Release other women from the obligation to maintain status quo groups. Let other women know they have your friendly encouragement and support as they seek new or more personally satisfying work situations.

* When a co-worker receives a promotion or goes to a new department, plan a lunch with her to show your support and interest in keeping alive your connection with her. Our networks will flourish if we continue to extend our connections throughout all levels of the workplace.

3

Showing
We
Care

Women bring to work what we learned at home—and one component of that knowledge is how to care for and about others. Kathryn Kastama, adult education instructor in Berkeley, California, describes it this way: "A woman's ability to express caring supports the work she does. Women notice the whole person; we are attuned to other women's mental and physical well-being. My students respect my professional skills and I respect their commitment to learning. They notice if I look tired or seem distracted. They encourage me to take time for myself away from school, to relax and revitalize. I offer them the same respect and concern. Caring becomes the base for the work we accomplish together."

Kathryn's experience parallels what women in all work situations know: caring matters to us. We need caring to be and to give our best. Caring goes deeper than connecting. When we care about other women, we concern ourselves with their feelings. We acknowledge the importance of positive self-worth to job satisfaction and performance. We encourage personal growth and reward accomplishments with recognition for jobs well done.

Most of us experience caring when we work with women. In our survey, more than two-thirds of the women responded "women understand" when we asked what they appreciated about working with women. Another third went on to add that "women care." They told us that women "show concern," "are compassionate," "sympathetic," and "sensitive." They noted that women "take time," "encourage," "nurture," and "express appreciation."

Women's desire for caring is so strong that it often is a determining factor in whether we enjoy where we work. As author Deborah Tannen notes in *McCall's*, "The feeling that the people they work with are interested in them personally seems to be a requisite for many women to be happy in what they are doing."

But we don't only want to be cared about we also want to take care of others at work. In her book on women's moral development, Carol Gilligan concludes that women feel a "moral imperative" to care for others. And what we expect of ourselves—that we will provide caring—we expect of other women whom we understand to share our values.

The Benefits of Our Caring

Caring deepens our commitment to other women and provides a vehicle for support, encouragement, and recognition of our worth. When offered appropriately, caring can enhance a workplace environment, making people feel welcome and appreciated. When no one seems to care or caring is offered inappropriately, it can debilitate women and destroy our productivity and job satisfaction.

How do women express caring? First, we listen. We offer others our time and attention so we can learn about their feelings and appreciate their thinking. Caring means taking time to listen, and hearing what someone says. Deborah Tannen makes a comparison between female and male communication styles. Women, she tells us, listen. Men lecture. Listening means paying attention to what the other person says and then responding with complementary conversation that affirms the other person's value and says we have heard her concerns. In contrast, lecturing begins with the unspoken: "You've had your say, now this is what I want to tell you about me."

In *The Female Advantage: Women's Ways of Leadership*, Sally Helgesen identifies characteristics shared by the successful managerial women she studied. All of these women were willing to accept unscheduled interruptions during their work day and take time to listen to people. "Caring. Being involved. Helping. Being responsible. These were reasons the women in the diary study gave for spending time with people who were not scheduled into their day, and whose concerns may only tangentially have affected their immediate business," writes Helgesen. Making themselves available reflects, Helgesen tells us, the emphasis these women put on relationships and keeping those relationships in good repair.

Listening gives us a base for caring about others. Listening lets us know our co-workers and gives us an opportunity to encourage their self-worth and recognize their accomplishments. This is a crucially important female work trait. University of California-Irvine Professor Judy B. Rosener did a study of successful male and female managers. One difference between the male and female managerial styles Rosener observed is the value women place on enhancing the self-worth of co-workers and subordinates.

Rosener tells us the women discussed ways that they build a
feeling of self-worth in their co-workers and subordinates.
"They talked about giving others credit and praise and
sending small signals of recognition," Rosener reports, and
then adds that women make a point of acknowledging good
work by talking about it in front of others.

Women offer other women the caring and the recognition we know is crucial to self-esteem and confidence. Judith
Briles, in her book *The Confidence Factor*, documents the
importance of recognition to women's self-confidence, noting that the most essential area for increasing a woman's
confidence is recognition for a job well done.

Dr. Elnora Gilfoyle, provost and academic vice president at Colorado State University, is a woman who takes time
to enhance her staff's sense of self-worth by recognizing
their good work. One year during secretary's week, Dr.
Gilfoyle not only sent flowers to her department secretaries,
but she also wrote each woman an individual note thanking
her for her support during the year and mentioning specific
projects, instances, or events where she had made a special
contribution. At a meeting of Professional Secretaries International, everyone agreed that the women who worked with
Dr. Gilfoyle had received the finest recognition of all the
women present.

One group of successful career women expresses their
caring in a less formal way. These women work under
considerable pressure in the finance department of a large
corporation. They know their co-workers empathize with
their deadlines or are proud of their promotions when they
receive what they call "little givings." These notes of encouragement left on desks, gifts tossed over dividing walls, and
chocolate chip cookies in unusual wrappings communicate
that someone notices and cares. "Our ability to say we care,"
one of the women managers tells me, "is the 'great leveler'

among women. Managers encourage managers; support staff knows when one of us needs a boost; we can say thank you to our secretaries for extra effort."

Our willingness to listen and extend caring to all women regardless of status breaks down rigid hierarchical structures and replaces them with supportive relationship networks. A project supervisor shared this story as an example of caring that helped to build trust and rapport between a secretary and her supervisor. "Brooke came to work one morning with an ugly bruise on the side of her face," she told me. "We guessed she'd been abused by her husband, but we couldn't comfort her directly. Instead, two of us who had experience with abusive men let her know we were concerned about her injury. When I asked her if she was sure she was okay, she told me what had really happened. I listened. I didn't try to tell her what to do, but I did share what I had done the time I found myself involved with a man who hit me. The fact that we shared an experience brought us together and erased the difference in our job status.

"Because I cared, and another supervisor also listened and cared, Brooke felt safe talking about her experience. After she trusted that we understood each other and that neither my colleague nor I considered ourselves superior in this regard, she asked for our advice. Our caring, our willingness to offer support and listen, led her to seek help from a local program and move out of the relationship. Our caring supported Brooke in her personal life and also brought us together at work. Perhaps because we cared, Brooke is still with us. She is stronger as a person and our work relationships are stronger because caring has connected us."

When No One Cares

Caring matters so much to us that when we sense that those we work with don't care about us, we can feel used and often resentful. Clara is a good case in point. A senior administrative secretary for a metro area adult education program, Clara has a degree in history and economics. She was happy with her advancing responsibilities and salary until a new woman took over the director's position.

Charlotte, the new director, had no problem introducing herself to her staff in an outgoing "let me tell you about myself" manner. But she had no patience for listening to Clara or the other women when they wanted to share their experiences, feelings, or ideas for courses or procedures. Most serious for Clara, though, Charlotte seemed brutally uncaring when it came to telling Clara how to do her job. She criticized the scheduling system Clara had devised for rotating popular courses, and she never thanked Clara for assignments completed according to her instructions. She would simply take the printouts, say she would check them later, and outline the next project. Clara felt constantly reduced by the criticism and lack of recognition. Even when Charlotte adopted Clara's idea of course sequencing, a plan that increased registrations and made the program money, Clara received no thank you or note of appreciation. "I feel used," Clara told me. "Not even utilized."

I met Clara after her annual performance evaluation. Charlotte had listed all her inadequacies and mentioned none of her skills or accomplishments. With average or poor evaluations, Clara could lose her job, but she felt she had no motivation to make any improvements. "What's the use? I'll never get any recognition anyway," she complained. "I have performed well in the past. I know I am good at what I'm assigned to do and I contribute ideas that have improved our program. But I'm completely discouraged. This woman doesn't care who I am; she just wants a robot to get her work done." Clara saw no hope for the situation improving and was seriously looking into completing her teaching requirements and "getting out as soon as I can."

Sondra had already left her company when we met. She had started as a bookkeeper in the central office of a large grocery store chain. Over the years, she had completed an undergraduate degree and an MBA while working full-time. When she quit, she was making over $70,000 and had responsibility for the company's huge distribution system. "I left," she told me, "because all they cared about were my numbers, not me." No one had acknowledged how hard it must have been for her to earn her degrees and continue receiving promotions. No one had recognized the personal growth that had accompanied her increasing responsibilities. "The men I worked for told me they had recognized my accomplishments with promotions and salary increases. They didn't understand that I needed more."

When I last talked with Sondra, she had taken a position with a large charitable organization. She describes the woman director to whom she reports as "willing to acknowledge me as a person. She recognizes the challenges I accept and acknowledges how the results I produce relate to my personal sense of achievement. She cares."

Sondra's story illustrates how a company lost a valuable employee because those who worked there failed to exhibit a caring attitude. No matter what our work situation, we can offer each other support and caring—even when bosses or managers lack a caring style. We can acknowledge personal growth of our co-workers and show appreciation when they bring in a new client or impress a group of salespeople at a convention. And if we are supervisors and managers, we must remember to take time to balance criticism with appreciation for the person, not just for the performance. In doing so, we create an atmosphere in which we all want to work.

Care Betrayed

When we believe that other women care and then discover their caring is a hollow gesture, many of us react with anger and may seek revenge. Women seem especially vulnerable to this type of hurt because we seek relationships with other women and expect them to care. Men appear better able to walk away from a snub because they maintain greater personal distance. Men grow up competing for status, not relationships, and accept it when someone else plays the same game.

New to the business community, Linda and Paige opened a graphic design business in the same building where Arlene and Nan had been operating a successful marketing agency for five years. The two businesses cross-referenced clients, and Linda and Paige believed they shared more than just a fifth floor with their friends. Arlene and Nan stopped by to offer advice on everything from printers to press releases. They asked Linda how her children were holding up to her work schedule. They noticed when Paige looked tired and gave her the name of their massage therapist to help work out her tensions.

The new entrepreneurs accepted these gestures of caring from the older women until their first business lunch with the Chamber of Commerce. Pleased at recognizing familiar faces, Linda and Paige approached Arlene and Nan with extended hands and welcoming smiles. The successful duo, with averted eyes, passed by to exchange friendly greetings with business big cats. Linda and Paige were left with fading grins and cold, empty hands. Whether Arlene and Nan felt they would lose business opportunities if they stopped to chat with the newcomers or for some other reason, Linda and Paige were stunned and embarrassed. They had believed the previous caring gestures had connected them. When the older women ignored them, they got angry.

All of us can remember times, perhaps painfully, when we believed someone cared, but were ignored by her at a moment when a friendly act would have bolstered our self-esteem or eased a difficult situation. Close to 25 percent of the women answering our survey listed "betrayal" or "two-faced" behavior as one of their problems in working with women. "Care today, gone tomorrow" earns us the "two-faced" label. And we remember.

Eighteen months after the Chamber of Commerce meeting, Paige found herself in a position to recommend new members to an influential development board. Arlene's name appeared as a candidate. Reflecting that a person on this board had to help maintain good relations between business owners and city government, Paige voted against Arlene. If she could be so two-faced with Paige and Linda, might she not behave that way with others in the community? A less rational, but perhaps more heartfelt, explanation for Paige's vote might be "one good burn deserves another."

Caring gives us the basis for extending ourselves to others. But for caring to be the positive strength it can be for women, we must be respectful and consistent. When we act in a caring way, we set up expectations for trust. When that caring is sincere, trust bonds our working relationships and unites women. If the caring is insincere and we break that trust, we destroy the fabric that holds women together in a productive, mutually satisfying workplace community.

Out-of-Control Caring

When Mae West said too much of a good thing was wonderful, I doubt she had considered what out-of-control caring can mean for women at work. Though many of us thrive in a caring environment, unmonitored caring in the workplace has the potential to disrupt productive activity. "Many of us learned to value caring by watching our mothers and other women in caretaking roles," Barbara explains. "We can't easily turn off what we learned about being good women when we enter corporate territory." And that can create problems—particularly when we let our impulse to take care of others intrude on or distract us from our work priorities.

Barbara offers the story of Pam as an example. Pam had gone to Barbara for support during the breakup of her marriage. One of Pam's frustrations concerned a fellow travel agent, Loni, who was smothering Pam with caretaking. Pam felt she needed to separate her work and her private life, but Loni wouldn't let her. Loni had heard through her husband that Pam was recently separated. Loni tried to get Pam to talk about the situation, offering sympathy and insight from her sister's recent divorce. Pam, naturally a private person, resisted and tried to concentrate on her work. For Pam, work provided a healthy distraction from her personal problems. Also, a good performance had become more important than ever since she was going to have to support herself in the future.

Loni started leaving little trinkets with "keep smiling" notes on Pam's desk. Next she started sending supportive cards. By the time Pam went to see Barbara, Loni was offering to take over Pam's work for an afternoon so Pam could "enjoy the sunshine on these dark days." Loni pressured Pam to come over to her home for supper so Pam could "have someone to talk to." Pam complained to Barbara that she was being smothered with Loni's caring. Her work had slowed because of the time it took to respond to Loni's attentions, and the stress was becoming more than Pam could handle.

Barbara acknowledged that Loni's motivation to offer caring to another woman in crisis might have merit, but she also believed that Loni had inappropriately interrupted work time to indulge her own caretaking needs. Barbara helped Pam to understand that to end her stress at work, she had to confront Loni and tell her honestly that she appreciated her caring, but that she needed to be alone with her situation and to give her full attention to her clients while at work. Loni was hurt by Pam's "rejection" and felt confused that in trying to "be good" she had created rather than solved a problem. She responded defensively with "I was just trying to help." Later, Pam reported to Barbara that Loni no longer "bothered her," but that the lingering tension still disrupted Pam's concentration on her job.

A caretaker needs an object for her caring. Pam didn't let Loni know early on that she wanted to handle her personal situation alone, and, as a result, the caring became out of control. When a caretaker and a person needing care get together, a co-dependent relationship can develop that has potential to lure both parties into a quagmire of obligation and betrayal. "Caring is seldom unconditional," Barbara says. "When a woman expresses caring for another person, her expectations for that person go way up. She expects the other woman to reciprocate, and when she gets encouragement, her expectations escalate. It goes back to our belief that caring is good. And it is, when appropriate to workplace situations. But we create trouble when we expect our 'good behavior' to be rewarded. We assume those rewards will come as preferential treatment at work, and we set ourselves up to experience betrayal."

Some of us not only try to take care of each other; we also try to take care of the workplace and expect rewards in return. We have all known women in medical clinics, offices, bank departments, retail businesses, and every other field who feel responsible for taking care of everyone else. They make the coffee, arrange for birthday celebrations, collect money for flowers, and stay late to help produce slides. They make themselves available to cover for co-workers. They volunteer to shuttle children or provide airport transportation, even when the company provides these services.

In these situations, all may appear good-natured on the surface. Co-workers quickly adjust to the caretaking and the gestures often go unacknowledged. But the caretaker expects a return, and when she isn't rewarded with the transfer she wants or the promotion to a new classification, she feels resentful and betrayed. "We need to know," Barbara concludes, "that we don't have to always take care of others. We can all care about each other and share the caretaking. And we need to know that being good caretakers will not necessarily bring us work-related rewards. Our job performance and the business's needs come first."

The authors of *Megatrends for Women* reinforce Barbara's point. "Caring about people and supporting them," they write, "always must be balanced with objectivity." Women who care recognize the value of empowering others. "In certain cases," *Megatrends* concludes, "the way to empower someone may even be to fire them, express anger, impose strict discipline or have a knock-down, drag-out fight—a verbal one, that is."

In *Secrets Between Us: Women and Competition*, Laura Tracy tells the story of Mary Catherine. Mary Catherine, acting on her assumption of what would assure her tenure at a large university, relied on "pitching in" and helping with administrative tasks rather than concentrating on her own writing and research. "At the same time," Tracy writes, "Tamara, hired during the same month as Mary Catherine, concentrated on writing and publishing a book, refusing all optional administrative tasks that interfered with her writing time. In a competition for popularity, Mary Catherine was the hands-down winner. Her willingness to overburden herself made her enormously well-liked among her colleagues, while Tamara, although well-respected, was considered arrogant and overly ambitious."

When both women came up for tenure, though, Tamara received the appointment. Mary Catherine "'heard' the message that being a 'good girl' was more important than her own ambitions. Attempting to serve her colleagues, she failed to serve herself," notes Tracy. What Mary Catherine needed, Tracy concludes, was to create a boundary between herself and her workplace.

"Creating boundaries," Barbara adds, "may be one of the most important lessons caring women must learn to survive comfortably at work." Boundaries, as Barbara defines them, mean "that space between ourselves and other people that allows us to keep a definition of who we are." If we lose ourselves in caring for others or in allowing others to care for us, eventually we lose our objectivity and our ability to function effectively in response to workplace demands.

Caring Too Much May Hurt the Very Best

The caring that we exhibit in our relationships with others at work can be a powerful tool for encouraging personal growth in people we supervise or work with. Because we care, we get involved. We communicate about feelings as well as about work assignments and performance. We know people as individuals. We know what matters to them and what motivates them. When our caring focuses on helping others develop and succeed, how could there possibly be a problem?

Problems occur when a caring woman becomes too involved supporting and protecting those she wants to encourage. Men working with women seem to maintain a distance and independence that discourages overprotection. Women, on the other hand, feel more comfortable with personal connections and respond to caretaking with familiarity and appreciation. When we, as caretakers, don't restrict the limits of our protection and support, we can deny those women we have nurtured the opportunity to learn, fail, grow strong, and succeed without us.

Ardis, a forty-three-year-old product marketing manager who supervises writers and marketing engineers, acknowledges one of her weaknesses is "caring to the extreme. I care about people," she told me, "especially young women who need support in order to develop the self-esteem they must have to succeed. I spend a lot of time working with people to help them overcome their shortcomings. Often too much time. As long as I continue to support these people, they'll do okay. I'll be there to intercede, to solve problems.

"The problem comes," Ardis honestly admits, "when a woman I have supported becomes dependent on my caring and help and can't survive on her own when she is transferred to another area." Tasha had been in Ardis's department and confirmed that Ardis's caring, though supportive and welcome at the time, had made it hard for her when she was transferred to a new product team. "I didn't even know what I didn't know!" Tasha told me. "I floundered, trying to figure out how to work on my own. When I asked for help from my new manager, she gave me specific tasks and guidelines for accomplishing them. I worked hard, researching the information I needed and pulling together the activity. I felt pressure, but also satisfaction in learning that I could produce on my own. Ardis cared, but she didn't make me take responsibility for myself. Caring doesn't only mean helping. Caring can also mean letting someone become independent."

Ardis relates her caretaking to a "need to rescue anyone in trouble." She also acknowledges that she has difficulty criticizing or discouraging others. "She always sees the best in the women she's encouraging," a woman who has worked with Ardis explains. "She doesn't worry about what they are lacking. She doesn't confront their weaknesses. When they move on to other managers, the new managers aren't as tolerant." One woman who had been in Ardis's area and is now in another department expresses her frustration at not having been evaluated accurately by Ardis. "I always used to be okay," she complains. "Now I'm not, and I've lost precious time when I could have been learning."

Ardis recognizes the problem she has with limiting her caretaking impulses. She sincerely cares about the women she can help develop for success, and she doesn't want to weaken their opportunities. "The challenge for me," Ardis admits, "is to let someone fail. I spend much more time than other managers trying to develop a woman before I accept she is a lost cause. Even then, it is hard to let go."

Ardis recognizes part of her problem comes from her discomfort confronting conflict and delivering criticism. Ardis has been successful herself and knows she is in a position to mentor bright, young women moving up in her corporation. She has requested coaching in both areas so she can balance her caring impulses with the responsibility she has to properly prepare these promising women for their futures.

Leslie Botha is a self-aware woman who believes her inability to limit her caring impulses contributed to the failure of her magazine, *Changing Woman*. However, unlike Ardis, who restricts her caretaking to work-related situations, Leslie extended her caring to the personal lives of her staff.

"Especially since we were a magazine dedicated to women," Leslie remembers, "I believed it was important for us to know and care about each other—beyond the abilities we brought to the business. I felt it was necessary for us to take time out of the schedule to talk about our lives. We formed a support group for each other as we pursued our goal of creating a national magazine that carried a positive message for women. Much of what we shared with each other concerned family issues and our relationships with husbands and the men in our lives. I soon realized I was in conflict. I cared about the personal lives of the women I worked with, but taking time to talk at work took time away from business, meeting deadlines, and, in fact, from making money.

"Then one of my staff found herself in a dirty divorce situation. She needed to talk through all her hurt and anger. She began coming into the office at night and sleeping on the couch. Because I cared that she needed support, I would leave my own family and come in at night and listen. That didn't make the days any easier. She didn't make the distinction between work time and personal time. She saw her personal need as primary, and she saw me as the person who would take care of her. When I had to pull away, to say that during work hours work came first, she felt betrayed and took her anger out on me and the business. Because of the time she demanded, we missed a series of deadlines, lost concentration on our focus, and began what became the end of a very promising publishing experience."

Now a radio talk show host and newsperson in Estes Park, Colorado, Leslie plans to apply her experience when she returns to publishing. "I've learned," Leslie reflects, "from the distance of two years. I am a woman. I care about women and about women's stories. And, when I start up

Changing Woman again, I will manage the work hours differently. Our personal sharing will happen *after* we have met the deadlines and covered the bills. I will monitor a strict balance between caring about people and caring about getting the job done."

As Leslie notes, to assure that our caring about others remains an advantage of our feminine style, women must achieve a balance between caring for one another and doing what needs to be done. By doing so, what we have to give and what we can receive will truly enhance the workplace for all of us.

Men who have learned more about fending for themselves than caring for others may be slow in recognizing the value of a caring workplace as a positive environment for everyone. Women have the opportunity to teach men how to integrate caring into the goals of performance and productivity that will always remain essential to business survival. Our expressions of caring can change the atmosphere of a workplace from one where women feel like machines to one where we know we are part of a caring community. The caring we bring and the caring we express are important factors in creating comfortable and supportive workplaces for the 21st century.

Suggestions for Constructive Caring

* Show respect and caring for the feelings and self-worth of other women. When you notice that someone seems distracted or unusually emotional at work, let her know you are available to listen and offer support. But do not intrude if she doesn't respond to your caring. Honor her personal boundaries for privacy.

* Understand that you are not expected to take care of everyone at work and that it is not the first responsibility of

the workplace to take care of you.

* Make a point to acknowledge to other women that you notice their talents and contributions at work. This doesn't have to be a formal process. Stopping by a desk or jotting a hand-written note is all it takes. If Tamara presents an excellent annual report or Annette delivers an effective presentation, make sure you refer to specifics of their performance when you recognize their work.

* Remember that caring can also mean a willingness to give honest, constructive criticism. Sometimes our co-workers need to hear criticism and even face failure in order to grow personally and professionally. We cannot let our caring impulses compromise our responsibility to be objective about workplace priorities. Caring isn't protecting—when we care, we empower other women by giving them the criticism, the information, and the support they need to succeed.

* If you find you have trouble balancing your caretaking needs with workplace demands, consider reading Melanie Beatty's *Co-Dependent No More*. This classic book on co-dependency gives insights into how to break destructive relationship patterns.

4

Creating
Competence

Working women are good at what they do, but we don't always accept that reality. We often battle low self-esteem and the challenge of "learned helplessness." (In *The Female Advantage*, Sally Helgesen observes that it takes a woman five years longer than a man to acknowledge she is good at what she does.) Some of us avoid taking risks to protect ourselves from the devastating prospect of failure. And those of us who lack confidence in ourselves tend, according to Barbara, to "project our concerns about our own competence onto other women." Since we know our own weaknesses so well, we assume other women must have similar weaknesses too.

But when women recognize and encourage the competence of other women and when we accept our own strengths and worth, we create a comfort zone for competence, a place from which we can assume our real power in the world. We need this place, for the more time we spend there, the more the competence zone feels like home.

We *Are* Good

Ruth, a young Ph.D., worked in a solar laboratory at a large midwestern university. She watched the lab population shift as researchers, graduate students, and assistants of both genders came and went. Ruth realized that she appreciated working with women because female scientists "had prepared well, cared about the lab as a whole, and were committed to being the best."

Her experience with women's demonstrated competence supports what our success in school and at work has proven. We are good; we are very good. In ninety separate responses, women answering our survey mentioned competence as a positive factor in women-working-with-women situations. They said women "do the job well," "can accomplish anything," "are conscientious," "hard working," "well prepared," and "aim to achieve."

Louise McCoy, former assistant dean of women at Sonoma State University and currently a successful business owner, speaks for many of us when she says, "I expect a woman to be competent, more than competent, when I hire her for my business. I know how good she's had to be to prove herself in other jobs. I count on women, and I have not been wrong."

Louise's comment echoes the belief that, in fact, women have to be more competent to succeed in business than do men. In *The Compendium of American Public Opinion*, Dennis A. Gilbert quotes the results of the 1985 Virginia Slims American Women's Opinion Poll. According to that poll, 77 percent of American women agree that "to get ahead in this world a woman has to be much better at what she does than a man does." Of that 77 percent, 47 percent agree strongly.

When we look at how our competence affects our

achievements, we can be proud. When *Fortune* magazine asked a group of CEOs in 1992 how the situation for women had changed in their companies over the past five years, the CEOs reported a 92 percent increase in female managers and a 62 percent increase in female corporate officers. "If you look at the ranks of any major corporation below the top twenty people," says Lester Korn of Korn/Ferry International, "you'll find that 50 percent of the next group of managers are women."

More women are also seeking an education that will aid them in further developing the competence they will bring into the workplace. Today, women represent 33 percent of all MBA students. By 1998, more than half of the doctorate degrees awarded in this country will be granted to women. Women comprise close to 50 percent of the students at Harvard, Yale, and Stanford. Twenty percent of all engineering students are women, and women represent 38 percent of the students at M.I.T.

As all these statistics show, women are competent. We work hard. We have shown we can do well. So what holds some of us back from full achievement? The problem for women, and for women who work with women, isn't that we lack skills and abilities, but that we don't always trust our competence. Not *one* woman who completed our survey said that women weren't good at their work. Many, however, told us that women they worked with had low self-confidence, were "insecure," "felt inadequate," or "were afraid of taking chances."

The fear of not being competent can terrify, even paralyze, a woman. Her need for others to recognize her competence can dominate how she decides to act and when she chooses to take risks. Because of this, many women hold themselves back from advancing in their jobs and careers. And when we hold ourselves back, we deny other women a model for accomplishment and success. We also deprive our partners, business associates, and corporations the full advantage of our talents and abilities.

Learned Helplessness

"A critical breakdown of will to master difficult and risky situations remains at the core of FEMALE experience," Nicky Marone writes in her insightful and practical book, *Women and Risk: A Guide to Overcoming Learned Helplessness*. Marone describes learned helplessness as a self-defeating condition which keeps many women from confronting risk and benefiting from opportunity. "Learned helplessness," according to Marone, "ensnares a woman in a tangled web of paralyzing beliefs, emotions, and behaviors. She consistently doubts herself even when she performs at consistently high levels. Superior achievement in one area of her life does not necessarily translate into high self-esteem or promote self-confidence in other areas. Criticism can so immobilize her with its implication of inferiority (which she already believes anyway) that she may scrupulously avoid new challenges, risks, or changes that involve possible confusion or even the potential for negative criticism. Fear and self-doubt short-circuit her attempts at change. Worst of all, she eventually becomes blind to genuine opportunities."

Of course, not all women carry the burden of learned helplessness. If we do, however, we may be hampering our own success—and modeling behaviors that could threaten other women's potential to succeed. Marone believes women don't have to remain stuck forever in the grip of learned helplessness. We have an alternative, she says, by developing a mastery orientation. We can do so, she believes, by substituting performance goals with learning goals.

Women who feel more comfortable with performance

goals than learning goals limit themselves to activity in areas where they have already proven themselves competent. They're more interested in performing well than in learning something new. Some teachers, for example, choose to remain in the classroom where they know they perform well rather than prepare for administrative positions where they aren't certain they will succeed. This inclination to keep doing only what one is already good at perpetuates the status quo and impairs functioning in the face of adversity or challenge. This type of thinking, writes Marone, this notion that "to achieve a high level of ability, I must already have a high level of ability," is about as useful as "dehydrated water."

At the other end of the spectrum are women who choose learning goals. These women are mastery-oriented. They seek and accept transfers to new areas in their corporations. They expand their skill base as trainers to include new team-building concepts. They learn how to facilitate groups and approach new organizations and companies. In other words, they constantly seek opportunities to learn new things. And rather than attribute failure to their innate inadequacies, these women tell themselves, "If that didn't work, I'll try something else." The mastery-oriented woman focuses on the future and solutions rather than on past failures and inadequacies.

I originally approached starting a business with a performance-goal style. I felt comfortable repeating what I knew, which meant editing academic papers and teaching basic college composition. After my partner and I began our business-writing workshops, I would blame myself and be miserable for days if every manager and project leader didn't give me a top evaluation at the end of the workshop. My inclination was to go back to the university and teach composition forever.

My partner, Betty, on the other hand, has a more mastery-oriented approach. She saw—and still sees—every challenge as an opportunity to learn. She focuses on the new territory she has conquered, be it an innovative program to guide teams in writing procedures or facilitating groups in developing mission statements. If a program doesn't receive 100 percent rave reviews the first time, she doesn't dwell on blaming herself but instead asks why things went wrong and brainstorms how to improve the situation.

Recently an international company asked her to develop a seminar for their clinical liaisons. Rather than hesitate because she had never worked with a similar group before, Betty saw the opportunity as a great chance to learn something new. The program wasn't a perfect success and Betty decided to investigate why. She never doubted her ability to develop and deliver a good workshop, so she looked for external factors that might have influenced the results. She realized that the audience description she had received did not match the group that appeared for the seminar. Then she read the course description the participants had received. The program announcement suggested topics and format very different from the proposal she had submitted! Betty determined in the future to ask more questions about who would be attending her workshops, and she made a firm policy to see and approve course descriptions before they were announced to prospective participants. As a result of not succumbing to a perceived loss of self-worth, Betty improved her competence and her likelihood of future success.

Betty and I are partners. If I had stayed in my learned-helplessness mode, I doubt if our business could have grown as successfully as it has. But I have learned from Betty and from Nicky Marone to be more mastery-oriented, and now I am involved in *two* successful businesses. Three years ago if anyone had suggested I write this book, I might have said, "How can I do that? I have never written a book before!" (And thought to myself "I might fail and feel worthless and miserable.") But with my added confidence, I agreed to write this book and figured I would learn as I went. Whether it saw print or not, I knew I would learn more about women and about a process that would help me with future clients.

We as women will hold our partners and our businesses back if we remain stuck in a learned helplessness mode. As Betty did with me, we can encourage each other to break old patterns and master the future. We owe it to ourselves. As we become more mastery oriented, the rewards will follow. Our anxieties about competence will decrease as our esteem and confidence increase. Our achievements will be our incentive and our goals will have no limits.

Risking Risk

Betty and other mastery-oriented women model the approach we need to take if we are to welcome challenges that will expand our competence. Mastery-oriented women tend to be risktakers. They assess the situations, know when they are ready to move on, and concentrate on learning rather than repeating past performance. Taking risks doesn't mean foolishly leaping to take on responsibilities for which we have no training or aptitude. Taking risks means knowing our strengths and being willing to stretch beyond the comfort zone of proven competence to take on new challenges and responsibilities. Calculating risk involves assessing our chances for success, and moving ahead when the odds look in our favor.

Healthy risktaking applies to both successful entrepreneurship and advancement in the professions. *Breaking the Glass Ceiling* co-author Ann Morrison talked about risk during the American Management Association's First Annual Conference for Working Women, "Leadership for the '90s," in October of 1992. She repeatedly emphasized that women must be willing to take risks if they are to get ahead in a corporate environment, as entrepreneurs, or in the professions.

Betty and I learned this lesson early. Our tendency, shared with many women, to over-prepare before taking a risk could have held us back while more confident trainers were getting their feet in the corporate doors. When Betty and I first started our communications training business, we happened upon an article in an airline magazine that talked about women who refuse to take on new responsibilities or learn new jobs because they believed they lack education or skills. Many men, in contrast, leap at chances to prove themselves. They say yes to opportunity and pick up the skills they need as they learn the new job or position.

That point really hit home for me! Betty and I had just signed up for our third seminar on business writing, even though we had taught writing at the university for years! We felt we had to know everything about writing and pass every possible test before we could offer our skills to paying clients. The article had us pegged. We were stuck in the rut of over-preparing rather than taking the necessary leap to begin our own workshops. That article gave us just the kick to get going. We stopped studying and started marketing. Within three months we had contracts for workshops on performance evaluations, procedure writing, and newsletter editing. What we knew made us competent to begin; the rest we learned from experience.

Some women realize early that studying isn't the only way to prepare for risk. Experience has value too. I met Deb, a process manager, described by one of her colleagues as "a highly competent woman, a risktaker who serves as an example for many of us." I asked her about her approach to risktaking. She told me that at one point she felt she could advance no further with her corporation because everyone in positions above hers had engineering degrees and she did not. But then she assessed the skills required for the job at the next level, and determined that she really didn't have to be an engineer. "Maybe I didn't know everything an engineer would know," she told me, "but I knew where to begin and I knew how much I could learn."

Deb went ahead and applied for the promotion. Today she is the only non-engineer manager for purchasing in her division. However, she will probably not seek her next promotion in an engineering-related area. "I know my strengths and I know my limits," she concluded. "I am not an engineer and I don't want to go back to school to become one. I am, however, an excellent manager of engineers. That's where my strength lies. When an opportunity comes to challenge my management skills, that's the direction I will take."

Deb adds that women need to know we don't have to be locked into a situation because we don't have a particular degree or credential. We need to accept what we know and believe in our abilities to learn new skills as necessary. As she said during our conversation, "How can we know what we can do if we don't take risks?"

Opportunity will not always come looking for us. Deb had to approach her manager and ask to be considered for the promotion. Because she isn't an engineer, no one had thought of her for the position.

Asserting ourselves can be difficult for women. We often wait to be noticed and tapped for promotion based on our competence and results. We want to believe that business plays fair and will acknowledge when we are capable of new challenges. But that's not the way the work world operates.

In *Success and Betrayal*, Hardesty and Jacobs refer to

"the Myth of Meritocracy" that has left some highly competent women feeling betrayed by organizations that have not noticed and promoted them. "The quest for the holy grail of individual recognition and irreplaceability leads naturally to the assumption that skilled performance will get you there," they write. "The myth that recognition rewards achievement is one of the most potent and pervasive among women at all levels within the corporate hierarchy. For many women, their belief in an operative meritocracy began in school, where talent and hard work were always rewarded, and that belief persists against all odds." Men, Hardesty and Jacobs tell us, reject that belief early and instead embrace and thrive on gamesmanship. But, "in the mythic meritocracy that women carry about in their heads, women work hard to be chosen . . . and then they wait. And wait."

It's time for us to assert our competence. As Hugh McColl, Jr., CEO of NationsBank told *Fortune* magazine, "Women have to push harder. They often feel that things will be done fairly, whereas men don't believe that, and in reality it's often not the case. So women must ask their bosses what's needed to get to the next level. Then they need to make sure they get those opportunities and ask for feedback every step of the way."

As McCall notes, competence alone will not assure us notice. We need to aggressively seek opportunity and make ourselves visible when opportunities present themselves. Mary Herbert talks extensively with her female colleagues about their careers. She tells them: "You have to go to management and say 'Here's what I think I can do; here's why; let me try it.'"

All women should heed Herbert's advice. We have to take charge of ourselves because no one else will. We need to know our strengths, find out what opportunities exist, and be willing to risk for what we want.

When We Risk, We May Fail

When we take risks, we always confront the possibility of failure. Indeed, failure can happen—and we need to learn that it's okay. Having failed gives evidence that we tried and that we're learning. But often women don't see failure this way.

Someone once told me that men wear their failures like badges to prove they've taken risks. But women often hide their failures, and sometimes themselves, after they have failed. Indeed, some of us feel so wretched about ourselves when we fail that our self-esteem and sense of worth plummets close to zero.

Nicole, a financial analyst in New York, lost her job after the 1987 stock market crash. Though it was not her fault her firm had to eliminate most of its staff, she internalized the failure and withdrew, literally, to her parents' home. There she felt safe from people who might ask what she was doing and what had happened to her promising career. Though one of the brightest students in her high school, she will not return for her ten-year reunion this year, five years after she lost her job, for she believes she let her female classmates down. "Women need to see success stories," Nicole says, "not evidence that we can fail."

Some of us, like Nicole, can't face others when we fail. And it's particularly difficult to face women who take our failure as confirmation of their worst fears about themselves. These women fear the taint of failure and the challenge to their sense of worth. Because of our fear, we lose valuable information about failure and the successes that can follow. Understanding our responses to failure can help us confront and overcome our discomfort.

In *Secrets Between Us: Women and Competition*, Laura Tracy offers insight on this issue. "Being serious about our work," she says, "means that failure is as serious as success. But women connect failure at work with failure experienced at home, where criticism usually is followed by emotional penalties, like withdrawal of affection or even abandonment. Unlike men, women often play an *emotional* zero-sum game at work—one loss makes us feel as if we are lost." Realizing we don't have to play this way can help us achieve the attitude we need to keep going and learning.

When Darlene and Josie gave up their jobs with the university to start a floral boutique, they did everything right. But the economy in 1989 was not kind and they couldn't keep the shop going without facing unmanageable losses. When a year later Darlene came to me for help with a resume, she told me that after their business failed, women they thought had been their friends at the university and in business groups withdrew from them as if they had a contagious disease.

"I never felt so alone," Darlene recounted. "Not only did I have to deal with the business failure, which I understood, but with rejection from other women which I did not understand. I believe women should support each other when we risk and fail, or we will discourage risk altogether. We can learn so much from each other. Withdrawing and rejecting are not the answers. We need to be there, and to help."

Darlene is right—we can be there for one another. Anita used the bankruptcy of her computer supply business as a growing experience for herself and other women. When the business she owned with her husband failed, she became depressed and wanted to leave town. She blamed herself, her lack of competence at business management, for the disaster. But her husband kept challenging her to accept the failure as a success. He reminded her how much they had learned, that they had sold over a million dollars in equipment and support services, and that they would recover.

Anita reassessed her reaction and realized other women might respond as she had. Those women needed her help. Anita became a counselor for other women who had taken risks and faced possible failure. She talked openly about her experience and what she had learned, forming a support network that helped Anita as well as the women she met.

Today she has a secure job with a Fortune 100 company working in international sales. When she knows of women who have failed on projects or assignments, she makes it a point to talk with them about what they have learned and what they will do next. "Women know how it feels for another woman to fail. We can't let these women isolate themselves, and we can't distance ourselves from them. We must support each other and share what we have learned. When we know women will support us when we have tried and failed, we will try more often. The more we try, the more we will succeed."

Ann Azari, elected mayor of Fort Collins, Colorado, models another way women can reach out and offer that support. Barbara had applied to serve on a development board, but she didn't receive the appointment. "Ordinarily," Barbara says, "I would have felt a sense of failure. My esteem would have been wounded and I might have vowed not to risk applying for such a position again. But Ann made the difference. She sought me out to tell me why I had not received the appointment. She said I was capable and competent, but that other applicants had more background in tax rules and other specialty areas the board would have to address. She didn't label me a failure, and she encouraged me to try again."

When we face hard times, we need more women like Ann to help us recover from failure and come back stronger and more confident than before. When women around us doubt their competence, it is up to us to provide much needed encouragement and support.

Competency and Decision-Making

One way we can encourage women's competence is to understand and support what some observers consider a feminine decision-making style. How a woman approaches decision-making suggests to us a good bit about her competence. If we see her to be decisive and firm when making decisions, we conclude she must be a competent woman. If she asks for everyone's input and then delays her decision because she still isn't sure, we conclude that she must doubt her judgement and her competence. That's because decision-making remains one area where many of us still look to the male model that believes "he who hesitates is lost." In this view, competent people make quick decisions independently, and deliver them with assertive confidence, whereas not-so-competent people take a lot of time to make a decision and don't decide without consulting others.

When we see women taking their time to make up their mind and consulting with a wide variety of people, some of us despair. We conclude that if she can't decide like a man does, she must not be as competent as a man. So we pressure her to hurry up, appear decisive, and not worry too much about the consequences. Yet a better approach for us would be to understand how women make decisions and to support each other where our style gives us strength and advantage.

To appreciate the feminine decision-making style, we need some background. Anne Moir and David Jessel, authors of *Brain Sex: The Real Difference Between Men and Women,* see decision-making (what they call "decision-taking") as an area where a woman's brain seems to put her at a disadvantage in a male-dominated work situation. In fact, though, discounting a woman's approach may waste "a potentially important asset."

According to Moir and Jessel, "men and women have

different approaches to decision-taking. For the female, it is a more complex business, because she is taking in more information and taking account of more factors than a male. A woman's strength, and her weakness, is her capacity to perceive, for example, the human dimension of a business decision. Her mind, with its greater sensitivity to personal and moral aspects, and the greater facility with which it connects the elements to be considered, makes the decision altogether more complex than it is for the man, who relies more on calculated, formulaic, deductive processes."

The male approach demands "blunt" decisions, and both men and women have come to equate blunt decisions with competence. However, taking time to deal with complex input doesn't mean we are indecisive or incompetent. We can decide and we do; we simply spend longer with the process.

Sylvia, who sells computer equipment, respects the way the women responsible for purchasing her products approach their decisions. "These women, with responsibility for large budgets and groups of people, ask me all kinds of technical questions. Then they hold meetings with their staffs and gather everyone's input. When they talk with me again, they'll have specific questions that reflect what they heard from the people they included in the process." Sylvia adds that the women she works with may take longer to decide which products or systems to buy, but once they do decide, they have their support in place. They have anticipated problems and made good decisions that, once made, can be implemented smoothly and successfully.

The way women make decisions reflects balance. When women make work decisions, we consider the impact on people as well as on budgets and products. And many of us prefer not to make decisions in isolation but to balance our own assessment of an issue with what others know or think.

For some women, though, insecurity about making the best decision creates more problems than advantage. The fear of making a mistake can affect our decision-making even more than the fear of looking indecisive. Lack of confidence becomes lack of competence. These women can't make a decision themselves. They ask others for ideas and opinions both to seek reassurance for themselves and to avoid committing themselves to one action or position that might prove less than perfect. Such a woman tends to approach other women to help resolve her indecisiveness because she assumes women will be more tolerant of her insecurity than men. She fears men might express impatience with her vacillation and need for reassurance. She trusts that women will be kinder and take the time to encourage her worth and support her decision-making process.

Rosalie's story provides an example of the problems an indecisive woman can create when she shares responsibility for mutual decisions. Nora had established a successful marketing business with an emphasis on designing full-range promotions for products and services. The business had grown beyond what Nora could handle alone. After much consideration, Nora decided to take on a partner. Rosalie had presented herself as bright and talented and the two women shared a creative vision and compatible creative approaches. All went well until the first major deadline. Rosalie couldn't settle on the details within the concept. She would run ideas by her friends outside work and support staff at the company. She would even ask the janitor and the grocer on the corner what they thought. The minute someone would say something like, "*I* would never use the word 'celebration,'" Rosalie would panic and come to Nora wanting to change the promotion concept!

Nora found herself spending more and more time reassuring Rosalie that Rosalie's ideas were good and that she should believe in what they had worked hard to produce. But Rosalie continued to vacillate, even calling Nora at midnight because she had just seen an advertisement and liked what they had done with color. Rosalie's reluctance to commit to a decision caused the company to extend deadlines and appear unsure of themselves.

Finally, Nora had to take charge. She made it clear to Rosalie that to stay in the business they had to decide on a concept and present it with confidence. "Too much input can reduce a creative idea to mush," Nora explained to me. "To keep a concept fresh we have to trust ourselves to act. We can always refine later, or start again. Women need to recognize this. We must be more willing to trust in our vision, and the vision of the women who work with us." In a creative business, there are no assurances. Nora had learned to trust herself; she could go forward because she could always make another decision to refine her original one.

Projecting Our Fears About Competence

A woman's attitude toward another woman's competence reflects her own sense of esteem and can profoundly affect the esteem of her co-workers and subordinates. Secure women expect and embrace competence in others. Unfortunately, insecure women fear being revealed as inadequate and project their negative expectation onto other women. "We do this with other women much more than we do with men," Barbara explains. "Because of our alikeness, we identify with other women. We tend to assume that what we as individuals experience must be experienced by all women. We say, 'If I am this way, she must be too.' When a woman feels confident and competent, she projects that expectation onto other women. When her esteem falls, however, so do her assumptions about other women's worth and ability."

Those who don't expect competence from other women can do great damage to our potential for achievement and our collective sense of worth.

I met Cara soon after she had separated from her wealthy and prominent young husband. She had a master's degree in fish and wildlife biology and had made significant contributions to habitat studies before her marriage. Though she stopped working at the lab when she became a wife and mother, Cara had continued making contributions to the community. She gave her time to girls' sports and built a model gymnastics training program involving ten schools and a group of fifty volunteers.

After Cara was separated and looking again for work, Barbara referred her to me for help on a resume and job-search package. When I asked Cara if she wanted to return to research, she said perhaps, but she qualified her response by adding that she would never work in a lab where there were "a bunch of women." I asked why. "They're just not good enough, and I want to work with competent people," she said. "You can't trust women in a lab situation. When there's trouble, they just fall apart."

I was stunned. Cara had worked with internationally-recognized women researchers. I didn't understand why suddenly she would be so negative about working with women. When I spoke with Barbara on the matter, she suggested I work with Cara on building self-esteem. Since Cara felt worthless and incapable in her personal life, she projected those feelings onto other women in work as well as personal situations. If she could come apart, so could they. She didn't like what was happening to her and wouldn't want to tolerate such a breakdown in another woman.

With Barbara's help, Cara regained her perspective and recovered her self-esteem. She became involved with women's outreach programs and, by sharing her experience, helped other women recognize and develop their strengths. Recently we heard that Cara had started a company making swimwear for young girls. She employs primarily women and plans to enter the international market.

Sometimes a woman who fears she is inadequate can project that insecurity onto co-workers, making them doubt their abilities and potential. Wanda worked as a clerical technician for a company that had recently purchased a new accounting system. She felt threatened by the change and feared she couldn't learn the new system. Wanda assumed the women she worked with wouldn't be able to learn the new system either. Her negative attitude proved contagious. The technicians stood united against learning the new system until Peg broke ranks and volunteered for the training. Her confidence that she could learn the system set her apart from Wanda and the gang, who literally stopped speaking to Peg during the working day.

This story has an interesting footnote. As a "reward" for learning the new system, Peg was assigned to train the others. They were resistant, and it was at that time we met Peg at a workshop. She shared her story with the group and asked for suggestions on how to get these resistant women to learn the new system. If they didn't, she told us, they would be replaced. We told her that building the self-esteem and confidence of these women was as important as the actual training.

Barbara advised Peg to focus on Wanda. Wanda had learned many new skills in her ten years with the company and Barbara suggested that Peg recognize Wanda's abilities and begin there to build her confidence. (Of course, the prospect of not having a job if she didn't accept the training provided some powerful motivation for Wanda as well!) When Wanda became convinced she could learn, she would assume the others could too. And once everyone had mastered the system, the whole group would feel more confident and positive about their competence.

In some circumstances, women project their fears backwards and question the competence of their subordinates and those new to their professions. Even those of us who have achieved still have doubts about our achievements. We ask ourselves, "Do I deserve to be here? Do I really know what I'm doing?" When we doubt ourselves, we can project our anxiety onto women who haven't made it yet. We resent their presence as a reminder of where we once were. These women represent who we might have been if we hadn't been "lucky." If one of them fails, it confirms that we could have failed and might still fail. In response to our fears, we test the competence of the women below us. If our subordinates handle the assignments and challenges well, we feel more secure.

Women who have built their career achievements on quality performance can be especially ruthless in their demands on the young women following behind them. Kathy Canclini, a nursing education director, draws an example from her profession. "Nurses," she says, quoting a term familiar to those in her field, "eat their young." Kathy goes on to explain that nurses work hard for their skills and positions, and waste no patience on nurturing new people who might not live up to their high expectations and subsequently threaten all they have accomplished. "They expect 100 percent from new nurses," Kathy says, "and aren't kind when they don't find it. Their motives may serve the profession, but aren't entirely without a self-protective aim. They fear that if other women can make mistakes, they could too. They don't feel comfortable questioning themselves."

When we question our competence and project our fears onto the women we work with, we do everyone a disservice. To stop this negative process, we must first be willing to recognize and accept our own worth. This includes our skills, our talents, and our ability to learn. Then we must agree to assume other women are as competent as we are, and to act on the assumption: competent until proven otherwise. Expecting the best often produces the best. When we expect competence, we build confidence. Confident women extend their belief in themselves to others, and create a competence comfort zone where all women benefit.

Too Much Competence?

A woman who appears highly competent or who has achieved high levels of success sometimes threatens other women. These insecure women need to be reassured that a woman can achieve and still retain her feminine values and behaviors. The successful woman may be a boss, an officer of our corporation, a leader in our profession, a rising star on the success track. Whatever her position, her visible competence attracts attention. As we've seen in previous chapters, if a woman makes an attempt to connect with other women and not hold herself distant and different, if she appears caring and inclusive, she may fare well and gain the support of her co-workers and subordinates. However, if she focuses primarily on dollars and products and disregards relationships with other women, she faces serious resistance and potential sabotage. In other words, if she behaves like a man, regardless of her success and prestige, some women will attack until they can "bring her into line."

Marjorie learned the hard way that not all women she worked with would support her just because she excelled in her position. When Marjorie joined an international male-dominated corporation she felt that proving her competence was all she would need to succeed. She had good ideas, proved highly capable with follow-through, took on added responsibility and moved ahead quickly. Then one day she looked around and realized the other women at her level and on whom she depended for information and support weren't there when she needed them. They had watched her star rise and, though they were stars too, disliked Marjorie's masculine drive-right-through and friendliness-be-damned style. "I'm not unfriendly," Marjorie wanted me to know. "I just become very focused and directive. I may not take time to listen to every feeling, but I certainly pay attention to ideas."

The other women, however, resented Marjorie's style. They felt like objects at Marjorie's disposal and rallied an attack. Their combined efforts at resisting Marjorie's demands for support took its toll. Marjorie feels she was sabotaged by the women whose competence she counted on for her success. She is angry that she won at the male game but failed with the women who played along side her. At this point, she feels it is too late to build the rapport she needs to work successfully within her current group. She has considered looking for another position, but the money she makes keeps her in place. Disillusioned and feeling betrayed, she has decided for now to work as independently as possible within the division, knowing full well that in so doing she removes herself from the fast track and the promise of the highest level of achievement.

When Myron heard we were working on a book about women working with women, he told us that his law partners and he would never take on another female associate. The only time they did, he told us, the other women in the office, the secretaries and paralegals, "just about destroyed her and the whole office."

Jane, twenty-five and fresh out of law school, wanted to appear as professional as possible. She had been at the top of her class in environmental law and believed that to continue succeeding, she had to keep proving herself with performance and not be distracted by the women in the office who were there to support her. She made the women feel like "underlings" and made it clear that her competence made her superior. The women expressed their resistance by giving her work the lowest priority, being rude to her clients, gossiping about her lifestyle, and expressing their opinion of her at social and public gatherings. She held tight to her convictions and made it clear her stature as an attorney separated her from the other women. The office became a net of tensions. The men had no idea how to intervene in the woman-to-women conflict but did identify Jane as the problem. Within the year she was asked to take her skills elsewhere. Unfortunate for Jane, for the firm who lost a highly competent young lawyer, and for the women who perpetuated the destructive image that "women just can't work together."

The central challenge, then, for competent and successful women lies in the implied threat they represent to women's expectations for other women. Seeing a woman in a position of authority threatens other women's sense of themselves as feminine. "I still believe," Barbara adds, "that some women fear success not because they are afraid they will fail, but because competence has been defined as a male domain. Being competent means appearing less feminine, and some women perceive appearing masculine as undesirable. These women project their fear about success and competence onto other women."

How do women act on that fear? They respond by punishing women who seem to flaunt their competence at the expense of their femininity. They can't attack achievement and ability, so they attack her femininity to prove that women can't be both successful and feminine. A conversation I recently overheard at an airport is illustrative. A group of women were talking about Hillary Rodham Clinton. "Maybe she's one of the one hundred best lawyers in the country," one of them said, "but look at her stodgy clothes! And her daughter must really suffer having a mother who's more interested in her career than in her family. I call that kind of a woman selfish and unnatural." I wasn't interested in any more of their conversation.

We must challenge ourselves to get beyond this mentality and accept that women can be both competent and feminine. Women secure in their femininity have achieved great success in their organizations and professions. Their competence has not compromised their femininity. Recent reports tell us that the happiest career women are those with husbands and families. Perhaps this is one area where in fact we can have it all. We can be competent and feminine—and we must allow other women to be both as well.

Suggestions for Creating Competence

* Accept that you have earned your competence. Challenge yourself to take appropriate risks to advance your career and increase your work satisfaction. Understand that you don't have to know everything before you begin. You don't have to read before you start first grade. That's why you go to school! Say yes to opportunities and use your competence to learn and grow as you meet new challenges.

* Let both men and women know that you appreciate working with competent female co-workers and superiors. In the past, too often women despaired of working for or with other women. When we stereotype women as less competent than men, we become our own worst enemies. Evaluate women's performance and applaud loudly the excellence you discover.

* Don't let failure devastate you. Look at failure as evidence you took a chance, you tried. A person who never tackles new challenges never knows how much she can grow. If you fail, assess what you did well and where you can

improve your skills and experience to succeed next time. Don't withdraw from women if you fail, or withdraw from other women who have failed. We need to learn from each other how to succeed and how to recover when we do not.

* If you think you may be caught in the patterns of learned helplessness that affect many women in our culture, you can break the cycle. Nicky Marone's book *Women and Risk: A Guide to Overcoming Learned Helplessness* (St. Martin's Press, 1992) and Sue Patton Thoele's *The Courage to be Yourself: A Woman's Guide to Growing Beyond Emotional Dependence* (Conari Press, 1991) are good places to start. For additional background and help, also consider reading *Your Perfect Right: A Guide to Assertive Living* by Robert E. Alberti (Impact Publishers, Inc., 1990), *The Confidence Factor* by Judith Briles (Master Media Limited, 1990) and *Woulda, Coulda, Shoulda: Overcoming Regrets, Mistakes, and Missed Opportunities* by Dr. Arthur Freeman and Rose DeWolf (William Morrow, 1989).

5

Choosing
Cooperation

Mary works as a secretary/accountant for a Better Business Bureau. "I love working here," Mary tells me. "We're all women and it's really refreshing. Carole, my director, takes time to get everyone together to talk through decisions. We all know what's going on and work together. They don't look at me as inferior. They seem to realize that my contributions matter. They count on me. I count!"

What Mary is describing is a work situation most of us seek regardless of whom we work with—one in which every person's contribution is valued. Researchers who observe how women build relationship webs, or networks, at work often use the word "interdependence" to describe how the connections function. When people are interdependent, they rely on each other's input to get the job done. Everyone has value. Everyone contributes.

The core value from which such interdependence springs is cooperation, a value that most women hold in abundance. The need for cooperation at work extends naturally from our

need for connection with other women and our willingness
to express caring. Connection with others forms the foundation for cooperation; caring for others and their contributions
sustains cooperative working relationships. Cooperation affirms our connection with other women and creates the most
positive environment for women working together.

In our survey, more than one-third responded that one
thing they like about working with women is that women are
willing to cooperate. They tell us that women are "not
hierarchical," "will share the spotlight," and "see each other
as peers, not competitors." They say that women will "listen
to the ideas of others" and will "share knowledge, information, ideas, work load, and skills." They mention that women
will "adjust their ideas to arrive at a unanimous decision" and
would "rather agree than compete."

Women respond positively to a cooperative environment. We have valuable ideas, talents, and skills to contribute. To take advantage of this potential strength, we must
respect both sides of the equation: our own willingness to
participate and our commitment to respect the contribution
of others. Cooperation unites. It is our strength. We must
encourage participation and cooperation; then watch as our
power grows.

However, when we let cooperation become a goal in
itself, we threaten our performance and restrict our achievement. Proper management of the cooperation comfort zone
lies in the balance between cooperation and personal advancement. Women who can maintain this balance are the
ones who will lead us toward our powerful, collective future.

We Want to Cooperate

When Dr. Frances Conley, a professor of neurosurgery
at Stanford University, was asked by *Time* magazine in July

of 1991 how medicine would differ if it were controlled by women, she answered, "It would be far less dictatorial. It would be management by committee—by teamwork. Uniformly, my operating room is a team of women, and I believe this to be true of most women O.R.s. The people who work with me are respected, professional, and do a job. We are all doing a job to reach a common goal, and that is to take good care of that patient. I think the nurses feel as if they have tremendous self-worth when they are in my O.R. There are lots of pleases and thank yous. My operating room is a happy environment."

Many women in business and industry would agree with Dr. Conley and her staff that a cooperative environment is a happy environment. Recognizing team effort is as much ·an attitude as a technique for involving others in a system that values and responds to individual input. The Total Quality Management approach being implemented by many U.S. corporations today is essentially cooperative—it sees each individual as a resource for quality improvement. Companies are learning to build teams of participating workers who feel involved and valued in a future-focused workplace community.

Professor Judy Rosener writes in *Harvard Business Review* that "inclusion is at the core of interactive leadership," a style that "comes naturally" for the successful female managers she studied. These managers realized that "encouraging participation has benefits. For one thing, making it easy for people to express their ideas helps ensure that decisions reflect as much information as possible."

To one woman Rosener interviewed, Susan S. Elliott, president and founder of Systems Service Enterprises, asking people to participate "is just common sense." Elliott claims that her accountants are the ones with the information she doesn't have. She needs their input to create a good plan, and she asks for it.

However, a manager who sincerely believes in cooperation and participation must take special care to make certain that if she asks for cooperation, she follows through on advice. "Of course," Judy Rosener writes, "saying that you include others doesn't mean others necessarily feel included. The women [whom she studied for her leadership research] acknowledge the possibility that their efforts to draw people in may seem symbolic, so they try to avoid that perception by acting on the input they receive. They ask for suggestions before they reach their own conclusions, and they test—and sometimes change—particular decisions before they implement them. These women use participation to clarify their own views by thinking things through out loud and to ensure that they haven't overlooked an important consideration."

Mutual and effective cooperation offers women opportunities to develop and contribute our talents in a positive, inclusive environment. Unfortunately, because cooperation is so important to us, if we can't work cooperatively, many of us withdraw. Our talents go untapped and our strengths unrealized. Therefore, it is vital that we create healthy, cooperative environments.

The Price of Not Cooperating

What happens when women aren't included in the decision-making process or if we feel our input, when solicited, is ignored? The answer to both questions is that when women feel unimportant and uninvited, we back off. We withdraw. We keep our ideas and talents to ourselves or take them elsewhere. When opportunities for cooperating don't exist, many of us resist contributing our best efforts and settle for simply getting the job done. "Not including a woman, not asking for her cooperation, is like saying you have no relationship with her," Barbara explains. "If she doesn't feel connected, she feels useless and perhaps worthless. If you don't care, why should she?"

The attitude that results when women feel excluded from the process sets the scene for sabotage. We have talent, we have skills, we have the desire to work hard and contribute. When we believe the system doesn't value us, some of us strike back by reducing our productivity or not challenging ourselves to perform.

Margot, director of a drug treatment facility, called her staff together regularly to solicit input on allocating resources, scheduling staff, and marketing the program. While she listened to each person's input, she then decided alone how she wanted things done, and sent around memos and assignments. The women on staff felt abused and demeaned—why had she asked for their input if she were going to ignore it—and responded by arguing against the new orders and even refusing to follow the procedures for which they had had no input. Margot continued the game by telling them how much she appreciated their input. She assured them, saying "I hear you. We're a team. Everyone is a contributor here," but her actions spoke louder than her words. She continued to invite participation, then made unilateral decisions.

When they could no longer work under Margot's authoritative direction, Kay and the other staff women went to the corporation. The regional manager saw that the facility operations had suffered and saw Margot's uncompromising style as the problem. Not only was the staff arguing her edicts, they were withholding their best performance because they didn't feel valued. Productivity suffered and something had to be done to regain the staff's confidence and commitment.

Margot agreed to attend a series of seminars on team-building offered by the corporation. There she learned that it was okay to really listen to the other women's ideas, and to use those ideas to improve her functioning as a director. Once the staff believed they had a voice in decisions and actions, their commitment to the program increased, and the facility's performance improved.

If we participate in good faith and then find out we weren't included in the picture, we feel betrayed and angry. If again in good faith we contribute our ideas and suggestions, only to have the person who requested our input disregard it entirely, we become resentful and non-committed.

Often women who have trouble letting others participate fear losing control if they share responsibility. Realizing that the cooperation her manager espoused on their development team was a "sham and a fake" angered Ginger to the point that she went to the general manager and asked for a transfer, "even if it meant being side-railed."

Ginger couldn't tolerate working with a woman who pretended to want everyone's participation and to respect everyone's ideas and input, but never let the others see "the big picture. In essence, she let us believe we were all participating as a team, but she lied. She dribbled the work so we never had a sense of where we were going or why. She controlled all the decisions. She made fools of us. I felt betrayed, and I asked to get out. When I told her why I was leaving, she called me naive! I prefer to think of myself as aware and honest. I would never take advantage of women's willingness to give and share. I wouldn't want to be responsible for all that anger when they found out I had manipulated their trust."

Recently I attended an American Management Association by Satellite Secretaries' Briefing. As I listened to the speakers, I noticed a theme emerging as an undercurrent to the topic of how secretaries can move ahead in a changing work force. Secretaries, it seemed, weren't motivated to use their skills to move ahead if they didn't feel part of a team. One speaker, Cassandra Warren, a leading trainer for AMA's Padgett-Thompson Division, admonished support staff to create a cooperative environment, if the environment didn't already exist. Secretaries who feel their potential isn't challenged when they simply respond to orders can take it on themselves to establish a cooperative team.

Warren advised starting with the boss/secretary team. She suggested that secretaries ask their bosses what they need, offer ideas and information, and learn how the organizations they work for operate so they could participate more fully. I heard her say, in so many words, "Create your own cooperation comfort zone. You will be happier, and you will perform better when you feel you are participating as part of a team."

Sharing versus Withholding Information

We have heard it everywhere. People who research and write about women at work boil their conclusions down to lists of four, or six, or eight factors. "Women cooperate" makes the list every time, and "women share information and power" shows up consistently as a subcategory of cooperation or as a factor in itself.

Sharing information helps us maintain the feeling of symmetry, or alikeness, that women seek in our relationships with other women. "If women are focusing on connections," Tannen writes in *You Just Don't Understand*, "they will be motivated to minimize the difference in expertise. Since their goal is to maintain appearance of similarity and equal status, sharing knowledge helps even the score."

In *The Female Advantage*, Helgesen identifies scheduling "time for sharing information" as one of the eight characteristics of effective female leaders. "This impulse to share information," she writes, "seemed to derive from the women's concern with relationships."

As these two researchers note, sharing ideas and information brings us together. It supports unity and allows for cooperation. Withholding information, on the other hand, is one of the most powerful weapons women can use against other women. Not sharing goes against our expectations for women. Men, we have all heard, "manipulate communication" and somehow we accept this as part of the game. When women, who are supposed to be caring and cooperative, withhold information or refuse to share ideas, we see it as treachery.

"Women expect to trust other women," Barbara explains. "We expect ourselves to share openly and honestly and we expect that of other women. When a woman breaks that trust and manipulates what and when she will share, she destroys our confidence in her and leaves relationships in serious need of repair."

Though the ideal may be to share openly in a trusting environment, many of us have known and worked with women who use control of information to gain power. *Deceptive Distinctions* author Cynthia Fuchs Epstein had this to say about women and our willingness to share information: "Oh, please . . . just think of how Aunt Tilly always withholds the single most important ingredient in her apple pie recipe."

Aunt Tilly knew that withholding the important ingredient left her the only person who could produce the best pie and gain admiration and status in her family. Ginger's manager withheld information from her team so no one else could understand the whole situation and she could retain an insider's power. Ultimately, however, her approach destroyed the cooperation of and good working relationships within her team.

Members of a team can also destroy good cooperative relationships by withholding ideas or information from the group. Tina, a health care administrator, looks at women who won't share from the perspective of a team leader. She considers a woman who intentionally withholds information to be untrustworthy and destructive to team function. "I can sense when a woman isn't contributing all necessary information," she says. "I can also feel when a woman has a criticism of my policies but won't share her concerns. Both ways, withholding information or ideas destroys cooperation and creates tension on the staff. When someone holds back, you can't trust her. And ultimately you can't work comfortably with someone you don't trust. Eventually the patients suffer, and when that happens, we have to take action." That action for Tina means first a direct confrontation. If her staff member won't willingly share ideas or information, Tina feels she has grounds to dismiss her.

A woman who finds herself in charge of women who withhold information as a form of resistance faces a difficult challenge. Judy knew the challenge she faced when she accepted an offer to leave her job in Minneapolis and come to Denver where she would be responsible for overseeing the introduction of a new accounts management system. "I had been in that situation before," she recounted to Barbara. "I expected to be tested by the women who resented my authority and feared the new system would eliminate their jobs."

Judy needed essential account information from women in the Denver regional branch offices. Women who saw Judy as a threat refused to cooperate. Judy put their options on the line: "Deliver the information, cooperate, and support change or you will be replaced." The women still refused, and after two weeks Judy fired three of the managers.

It was at this point that Judy went to Barbara for help. "She felt ambivalent," Barbara explains. "Women are supposed to cooperate with each other, but she couldn't get these women on her side. Somehow she believed she had failed the women she fired, and she came to me wanting to know how to make amends! I assured Judy that she had acted appropriately, in respect to the reasons she had been hired. The other women had fought her role and her function the most effective way they knew how: withholding information and refusing to cooperate. They chose their game and lost. Judy owed them nothing."

Our expectations for cooperation and our belief in sharing set us up to feel betrayed when woman take advantage of our good faith. Louise believed that cooperation meant helping someone get through a bad time. Sharing, she assumed, meant passing on information essential for someone to fulfil her obligations and performance expectations. This is how Louise McCoy tells her story:

"While I was in the Peace Corps in Africa, Marian, one of my colleagues, came down with malaria. I continued to do my job and I covered for her—picked up the pieces, saw projects to completion. When she recuperated, she took all the credit. She might have thought this was a form of cooperation, but when I look back on it I see that she really was stealing. After Marian recuperated, she continued to use my accomplishments by not letting me know when meetings were scheduled. She withheld that information until after she had made her presentations and taken credit for my work. I left the Peace Corps with a sour feeling about how some women treat each other. Later she became a feminist and got a Ph.D., but she has yet to acknowledge that I covered for her or that the accomplishments she claimed as her own were mine."

Sharing is fundamental to a cooperative environment. Exchanging ideas and information strengthens the team by affirming the web of relationships that hold it together.

Without sharing and trust, relationships break down. For women who seek cooperation with others as a base for job satisfaction and performance, an absence of sharing can create an intolerable situation. One of the greatest strengths in women-to-women workplace relationships is our willingness and ability to share. When we can exchange what we think and what we know, we build a powerful resource for ourselves and for our future. We must make every effort to trust and to extend trust so this resource can expand. We have skills and talent to share. Together we are more powerful than alone.

Stalled in the Cooperation Zone

Women recognize the value of cooperation to keep a network of relationships alive and productive. However, our willingness to cooperate makes us vulnerable to abuses, sometimes intentional and sometimes the result of losing perspective on our priorities. I was surprised, for example, when I asked Jan, a production manager, how she felt about women's willingness to share information. "Sharing just about did me in," she responded. "I was willing to cooperate to the hilt, until I realized that Claire was using my generosity to gain advantage for herself."

Though Jan and Claire worked at parallel salary levels in the same division, they were not positioned to compete with each other for advancement. However, a feeling of competition existed for Claire. A detail-oriented person, Claire felt threatened by Jan's ability to read the organizational process, communicate with people from different areas, and move ahead on action plans. To slow Jan down, Claire repeatedly asked for charts and dollar analyses that really had little to do with Claire's, or Jan's, areas of responsibility. Not wanting to appear as if she were uncooperative, Jan spent many extra hours generating and sharing "worthless" information, time she could have spent pursuing new ideas and moving ahead on projects.

After months of obliging Claire, Jan realized she was being manipulated. Claire's requests kept Jan back from the front lines and reduced her visibility in their group. Jan began challenging Claire on the value of the information she requested. Claire's arguments lacked credibility, and Jan decided to ignore the requests to see if Claire would pursue her demands. She didn't. Though Jan emphasizes that she will never refuse to share information that would help support a project, she claims she will never again allow another women to compromise her potential just so she can appear cooperative.

How many other women have held themselves back to appear cooperative? How many of us have buried good ideas or stifled divergent thinking in the service of consensus? "Women expect decisions to be discussed first and made by consensus," Deborah Tannen reports. "They appreciate the discussion itself as evidence of involvement and communication."

Consensus is an extreme way to prove that we cooperate; to reach consensus, everyone must agree. Therein lies the problem. "I knowingly and even painfully stifled a suggestion," comments Paula, a software engineer, "when I felt my idea would be seen as competing with the other women on the project. I finally decided that to put my energy into cooperation in support of the direction we were going was better than creating a problem and interrupting the process."

An overcommitment to cooperation, specifically to consensus building, can certainly impede progress when women work together. Robyn directs a treatment program for batterers for which she recently received a $900,000 grant. Her experiences with young female staff members have led her to be concerned with women's expectations for cooperation and equal input. "They seem to believe that because we're all women and are supposed to act like equals, their suggestions for programs and procedures is as important as input from women who have been working with abusers for years, have advanced degrees, and have lived what they know."

Robyn contends that she wastes valuable time listening to these young women who can't respect that what they know is not equal to what their seniors know. She also wonders whether she is making the best decisions for her program when she tries to accommodate everyone's ideas and bring all the women into consensus. "I need to communicate to the young women," Robyn concludes, "that new perspectives challenge our thinking, but that in some cases experience carries more weight."

Robyn is learning to balance consensus-building with performance and accountability. So, in her own way, is Tessa. Tessa is not comfortable moving ahead until she believes everyone she works with agrees with her. "I simply cannot go ahead," Tessa tells me, "until I have everyone in the room with me. I can feel it if they aren't, even if they won't admit their opposition. This can take way too much time. I've held meetings that I intended to last for forty-five minutes go on for three, maybe four hours while we tried to achieve consensus. I have to keep a check on myself and not let getting everyone to agree become more important than finding the best way to achieve a goal."

Tessa recognizes the importance of learning not to let her need for consensus compromise important decision-making. For, regardless of our desire to cooperate, there are times when we must take a stand and move on our ideas and positions, independent of consensus, in pursuing what we think is best. That's also why we must not punish women who disrupt consensus. Instead, we should support their independence and cooperate in letting them express their views and test our thinking.

The Product or the Process?

Another challenge for women working together is to balance emphasis on process with focus on the product or final result. "The White Male System," writes Anne Wilson Schaef in her classic *Women's Reality*, "has a product-goal orientation. The ends almost always justify the means, and it does not matter how a goal is achieved just so long as it is. What counts are outcomes. Men are constantly arranging their lives into a series of goals. The Female System has a process orientation. A goal is less important than the process used to reach it."

Too much cooperation, however, in establishing and defining process can sometimes overwhelm the necessary focus on goals. We can become so mired in discussing and evaluating what we are doing that we risk never really getting anything done at all! A city Commission on Women, of which I am a member, had been drowning in process for months. We had become so focused on how to hear each other and how to proceed during meetings that we lost track of what we hoped to accomplish as advocates for women and advisors to the City Council. Personal issues and personality factors further impeded our progress. We were frustrated, and clearly we were stalled.

Fortunately, we recognized our situation and invited a facilitator to guide us through exercises designed to break the impasse. During the facilitation, we affirmed that we shared a common mission: to serve women's needs. We also discovered that we all wanted to concentrate on tasks at hand and that we valued the satisfaction of getting a job done.

Identifying a common vision gave a focus to our desire to cooperate. We spent time discussing the expectations we brought to the commission. We revisited our work plan that identified specific tasks, and took responsibility for creating action plans to accomplish our goals. And we agreed to establish ground rules for our meetings that would keep us on track and assure that we accomplished our agenda. Today we still pay attention to process, but we do so constructively and in relation to achieving our goals. We have a focus, we cooperate, and we're getting the work done.

Suggestions for Cooperation and Consensus Building

* Model cooperation in your working style, and invite other women to join you. If you are responsible for a work group, allow time to hear input from all the women on your team. Listen to what they say and let them know how their ideas affect your decisions and actions. In a cooperative, participatory workplace, each individual represents a valuable resource who must be respected and acknowledged for what she contributes.

* Respect deadlines and workplace goals. Especially when we work with predominately female groups, we must know when it's time to stop the process of collecting information and start focusing on action. Consider using an agenda with strict timelines. Build in enough time early in the agenda for everyone to connect with the process and with each other. Then move to decisions and action.

* Understand that not all people will be equally prepared to contribute in the decision-making process. Balance respect for a cooperative environment with time constraints and the need to gather the best information available.

* Don't let the desire to appear cooperative discourage

you or other women from contributing challenging or divergent ideas. Cooperating means working together to achieve
good results. We cannot let our comfort with consensus
compromise innovative thinking or reduce visionary ideas to
over-processed mush. Instead, we must cooperate in allowing all ideas to be heard and in supporting women who take
an independent stand.

Common Problems and Strategies for Coping

6

Confronting
Competition

Recently, I had lunch with seven newly-promoted male managers from a computer products company. The table conversation centered on who was headed where in the organization and how the competition would turn out. I seriously doubted a table of seven women managers would have been at ease discussing who would be competing with whom and how many would eventually "make the cut." Instead, we would be discovering who was doing what tasks, how someone had prepared herself for her position, or how she was managing her family and her job.

As this example demonstrates, women tend to be uncomfortable about competition. Many of us don't want to be in an atmosphere that emphasizes who's better than whom rather than how we can work well together. However, women must come to terms with competition if we are to survive and move ahead in our jobs and professions. For the reality of the business world is, the higher we get, the fewer the available positions.

Competition by any other name is still competition: for recognition, for opportunity, for jobs, for the power that comes with responsibility and position. Whether we are moving up the ladder in the old male hierarchical system, or advancing toward the center of a web that describes for some the new female system, we are pitting ourselves against one another. And somewhere along the way, one woman gets promoted while another stays behind.

Women tend to be uncomfortable with competition because we're afraid it will break the bonds of connection we strive to establish. Our challenge, therefore, is to find a way to compete that respects the cooperation we prefer while at the same time allowing, even supporting, positive competition that challenges us to be our best. This can be extremely difficult for women because competition emphasizes how we are different, not alike. Deborah Tannen, who writes about the importance of symmetry in women's relationships, looks back to when we were little girls and reluctant to appear better than other girls in our group. "Appearing better than others," she explains, "is a violation of the girls' egalitarian ethics: people are supposed to stress their connection and similarities."

Laura Tracy, author of *Secrets Between Us: Women and Competition*, agrees. She sees competition as leading to power and ambition which disrupt relationships—and this is not comfortable for women. "Traditionally," she writes, "power has been a sticky issue for women. Defined in the context of individual achievement, power has meant winning while others lose, and having power has been experienced as selfish."

Where boys learn to play with their enemies and compete with their friends, and to seek and enjoy the power that comes with winning, girls learn to make friends by bringing everyone together. Boys learn that competition is okay and valid; girls learn that cooperation makes people feel good and that competition separates us.

"The general rule is that American males are simply trained to win," says Alfie Kohn, writer on human behavior, education, and social theory. "The object, a boy soon gathers, is not to be liked but to be envied, not to reflect but to act, not to be part of a group but to distinguish himself from the others in that group." Kohn goes on to say that with boys, competition "appears in full-strength concentrate."

Mixed messages about competition are common for women, creating for us profoundly ambivalent feelings toward competition. On the one hand, we live in a male-dominated society that says, "Act like a man and you will succeed." On the other hand, we are told to act like girls and cooperate rather than try to beat someone out in quest of a prize. "It isn't that women fear success," Kohn argues, as much as we are "backing away from the prospect of having to beat other people." We want to succeed, but we don't want to compete. These conflicting feelings affect our responses to competitive situations and make it difficult for us to understand and accept competitive behavior in the women with whom we work.

Indeed, the women answering our survey resoundingly identify competition as a negative factor of working together. Of all the negative factors named, approximately 20 percent relate to competition. Women tell us their female co-workers exhibit "extreme, sometimes vengeful competition." They say women "will go to any extreme to undermine other women," that they want to "succeed at others' expense," "fight for control," and "will step on any toes to get what they want." Ironically, these responses come from the same pool of women who laud how women care about each other, support each other, and want to cooperate!

This attitude, I believe, reflects our profound uneasi-

ness with competition. We need to resolve this ambivalence
before we can function comfortably in a workplace that
frequently positions women to compete with other women
for promotions and advancement. A first step is for us to look
at ways women have approached competition in the past.
With this background, we can evaluate our options and
choose an approach that respects our interests while encouraging good working relationships among all women.

Refusing to Compete

Some women simply refuse to compete with women
they know and like. Shelley Espinosa, a former executive
secretary and author of *Working Solutions for Working
Secretaries*, points out that women who value relationships
over promotions will often refuse to compete if they think
that by competing they might hurt someone else. In an
interview, Shelley described for me a woman, Kitty, who
wouldn't compete with her friend at the brewery where they
worked because Kitty couldn't stand the thought of seeing
her friend's face if she got the job and her friend was left
behind.

Some women, Shelley says, won't compete if they feel
their co-workers need the promotion and the pay more than
they do. They aren't comfortable advancing at another
woman's expense and hold themselves back to let others get
ahead. Sadly, the woman who does get the promotion often
has no idea that her co-worker paved the way. The woman
who sacrifices herself this way seldom receives a thank you
or sees a reward for her non-competitive gesture.

Maureen was quite open with me about her refusal to
compete with a fellow teacher and friend. When a district-
level position for a curriculum coordinator opened, I asked
Maureen if she were going to apply. "I thought about it," she

answered, "but Diane has already applied and I couldn't do that to a friend." It turns out that Maureen and Diane had discussed the necessary qualifications for the position and that when Maureen realized she might have an advantage based on her Ph.D. work, she decided submitting her own application would be "unfair to Diane, who had already put in her application." Diane didn't encourage Maureen to apply anyway, and used Maureen's discomfort with competition to protect her own chances of being selected.

Diane did get the job and never expressed to Maureen that not having to go up against Maureen's credentials might have worked to her benefit. Maureen was disappointed that her generous gesture seemed to go unnoticed. In fact, Diane took on a superior attitude and the friends drifted apart. Maureen realized that by not competing, she had lost both a chance at a job she wanted and a friend. When a similar position became available, Maureen applied. She knew none of the other applicants and didn't have to confront the issue of competing with a friend. Though she says she has "learned her lesson" and would never hold back again, the anonymity of the competition did make the application process more comfortable. She won the position because she was the best candidate. The new district loves her and Maureen loves the challenges of her new job.

Luckily, Maureen's refusal to compete with Diane resulted in a positive conclusion. Too often women who refuse to compete lose opportunities and are left feeling betrayed and frustrated. We must learn to talk openly about our ambitions with our friends and co-workers while assuring them we will not withdraw our support if they compete with us and win. When we hold ourselves back, we model behavior for other women to follow. That's not fair to ourselves, and it is certainly not fair to our collective future.

Creating Distance to Compete

Some women who can't comfortably compete with friends or co-workers withdraw from relationships in order to depersonalize the situation. While this approach makes competing easier for the women involved, it can disrupt communication and compromise productivity within the whole group while the competitors wait to hear who won.

Dr. Adele Scheele describes such a situation in the November 1992 issue of *Working Woman*. For five years, a woman she calls Pam had worked with Suzanna in their bank's corporate division. When their department director was promoted to become vice president, both Pam and Suzanna applied for the department director's position. Immediately a distance developed between the two women who had earlier shared information and supported one another's success. When Pam asked Suzanna what ideas she had for a new project they would be working on together, Suzanna responded by saying, "I haven't thought much about it yet." In fact, Suzanna had been thinking hard about the project, and she had already turned in a three-page memo to the new vice-president on the subject!

Competing up-front means publicly promoting ourselves based on our skills, experiences, and abilities. When we feel insecure about competing with others and subsequently withhold information vital to the progress of our department, we compromise productivity for our own personal ends. Of course, Scheele reminds us, distancing ourselves from our co-workers may be an important step in the preparation for moving into a new supervisor-supervisee relationship. And watching out for our own interests is not always a bad thing. However, the goal is to fulfill our own ambitions without harming others or affecting the productivity or objectives of our work environment.

Sue, a product marketing manager, has experienced the distancing factor in competition and doesn't advocate this approach if we want to maintain a healthy, functioning workplace. "The women in my area have a wonderfully cooperative and helpful attitude when there are no promotions or opportunities for extra money involved," she tells me. "Women lobby for each other's ideas; the atmosphere is creative and supportive. But when a position becomes available that could mean a promotion for one of the group, the atmosphere changes.

"The last time this happened, half the applicants were women and half were men. The women became more competitive and less cooperative. They withdrew from each other and literally stopped talking. Information and ideas didn't flow. The atmosphere grew tense and, frankly, unpleasant. This didn't happen with the men who just kept working together as always, often commenting about who was applying for the promotion and what was going on with the process. The men seemed better prepared to depersonalize the situation and accept the competition as natural and necessary. Once I completed my reviews and made my selection for the position, everything settled back into a cooperative mode. Typically in these situations, it takes the women longer to reestablish a comfortable working atmosphere than it does the men. All in all, when a group of women are involved, the withdrawal response can cost valuable time on our projects."

In contrast, Jacqueline's approach to cooperation and distance provides a positive model of how familiarity does not have to make competition uncomfortable. Jacqueline and another woman are co-directors with International Testing and Training Programs for the Educational Testing Service. Though they have different areas of interest and expertise and though they are different ages (Jacqueline is fifty, her co-director thirty-five), these two women developed a friendly, sometimes chatty work relationship. However, once it became clear that one of the women would be selected to be director, Jacqueline withdrew from the relationship. "Now that we could both be competing for the director's position," Jacqueline tells me, "I am not as comfortable being around her. I've cut the casual chit-chat about what's going on with her family or who I saw over the weekend. But we continue to share information about our projects and maintain a good professional relationship. Our polite distance allows us to compete and carry on in a healthy, business-like manner. The distance shows we respect each other and wish not to make the situation painful or difficult. When one of us becomes director, we will continue the same professional relationship."

When we stop communicating entirely with our co-workers because we can't confront competition, we hurt ourselves and destroy productivity for everyone. When we accept competition and manage our distance from others to support the competitive process, we make a positive contribution to our workplace. We give other women the space they need to assess their preparedness and evaluate their choices and risks. Also, we give ourselves space to gather our strengths and go forward focusing on what we can contribute rather than whom we have to defeat.

Politics provides an excellent arena for women who appreciate the up-front openness that publicly states, "I'm competing and I want to win." Opposing political agendas provides a natural distancing. No need to pretend, for example, that pro-choice and anti-abortion people will compromise their positions to appear cooperative!

Colorado's Secretary of State, Natalie Meyer, speaking at a women's conference, cites the openness of competition as a factor that attracted her and other women like her to politics. She notes that political opponents aren't supposed to be friends. They may respect each other, but it is understood that they come from different camps. "Politics," she adds, "also provides a marvelous opportunity for women to support each other and cooperate toward accomplishing goals." Today we have forty-eight women Representatives in the U.S. Congress and six women Senators. We have watched them compete; now we can learn from them how they cooperate.

Going Underground

Despite the number of women entering politics, out-in-the-open public competition continues to leave many women uncomfortable. We believe that if we try to break ranks to get ahead, the other women we work with will resent and reject us. So we go underground: on the surface we pretend to be happy with the status quo, while at the same time we are planning to take every opportunity to move up.

It is these women, who conceal their ambitions and aren't up-front about their interests in a promotion, who have the most difficulty when they do advance and find themselves supervising their former co-workers. The co-workers they leave behind feel betrayed, and very likely hostile or angry. The promoted woman discovers she has created a credibility fracture than can take months to heal. Instead of building a support base while she openly shares her interest in promotion or a new position, this woman leaves in her wake the bitter taste of deception. It will be difficult for her to approach her surprised former co-workers and ask for their cooperation because they will be hesitant to trust her intentions. She pulled the wool over their eyes once, why not again?

An example of this situation comes from a county legal

office, but it can happen anywhere across and up the pay scale. I met the women from this office when the judge they work for, Carol, sent them to one of our seminars. Carol hoped the women would benefit from seeing their situation in a more objective light.

Julie, Nona, and Alison had worked together as clerks for two years and considered themselves a group. When a supervisory job opened, Nona, the youngest clerk in the office, announced her intentions to apply. Alison told Julie, in confidence, that Nona was wrong in "trying to move ahead so fast;" she was, after all, the newest member of the group and "owed them something" for the help they had given her "learning the ropes."

Julie already felt uncomfortable about competing with women she knew, and Alison's indictment of Nona reinforced her discomfort. Julie had been taking classes to improve her skills with the intention of eventually becoming an accountant with the county, but now she wasn't comfortable telling Alison or Nona that she was applying for the supervisory job as well. Instead, she kept her plans to herself and applied in secret. When Carol noticed the application and wished Julie well, Julie asked Carol to keep the information to herself. She didn't want, she said, "to disturb the office."

After Julie, based on her skills and excellent work record, did get the promotion, she couldn't face the others and isolated herself in her new office for a week, arranging her work space and meeting only with Carol and the other judges. Eventually, Julie had to ask Alison questions about a records system she had not used in her old job. Alison, however, never seemed to have time to help Julie. Julie began to realize she would have to bring the group together to discuss their new working relationship. She called a meeting, where Nona managed to be late and then disrupted the focus by complaining about minor office policies and asking questions about procedures that had been in place for months. Nona and Alison continued to avoid Julie, and work piled up undone.

Carol, who knew all the women involved, tried to get the women to talk about their hostility, but they were reluctant to "complain to the judge." When productivity was still stalled six weeks later, Carol sought our seminar as a means to break the impasse. Away from the county offices, the women were able to discuss their feelings about competition and cooperation. Julie shared her reasons for not being up front in her competition with Nona for the job, and she openly asked for help from Alison, who had expertise Julie lacked. The women agreed to put their grievances behind them and to get back to work, but the whole incident had cost them almost two months of productive time.

Sheila, a woman I met while teaching a certification course for supervisors, took an opposite approach. When she read an announcement for a shift supervisor position at the hospital where she worked, she immediately decided to apply. She wanted the challenge and the money. However, she had worked as a nurse for only four years and she lacked the training in supervision that the job required. Sheila read about the course I was teaching and asked other nurses if they wanted to attend with her. She made it very clear that she was applying for the position and encouraged others to apply along with her. No one joined her in taking the class, but Sheila shared what she learned and even distributed some of the handouts she received. When Sheila did become shift supervisor, she already had the support of the other nurses. She had demonstrated that she would openly share her ideas and information. Her group lost almost no time adjusting to their new supervisor who modeled a cooperative style they all appreciated—even while competing with them.

We create problems for ourselves and for our workplace when we aren't open about our ambitions. Letting others know when we have applied for a job or promotion gives them time to sort out their feelings and allows us to build the support we will need as we move ahead. There may always be those who resent us for challenging the status quo, but we would be delivering a greater disservice to them and to other women if we held ourselves back. We must move where our skills, needs, and ambitions take us. As we lead, acting openly and honestly, others will follow.

Before concluding this section, I must offer one disclaimer. Of course, we will sometimes become aware of opportunities, jobs, or promotions that have not come to others' attention. In those circumstances, it is expedient for us to act immediately and not to court competition that could compromise our chances. Luck, Oprah Winfrey and others remind us, means opportunity *plus* preparation. When we discover an opportunity and we are prepared, we should act.

Not advertising an opportunity makes good career sense. Not telling your colleague, Kim, that you heard a bank across town or a department down the hall has an opening isn't the same as acknowledging an opening and then not admitting you are applying. When you come with the good news that they offered you the position, Kim may not leap to her feet to applaud your savvy, but she will recover. You did not sabotage her or lie to her. You acted appropriately in your best interests. She will learn the distinction and be prepared in her turn to do the same.

Creating a Rival

One way a few women get around the problem of competing with friends is to see all co-workers and colleagues as enemies. We usually don't feel ambivalent about competing with a friend when no pretense of friendship exists. So choosing to see another woman as a rival clears the way for "no-holds-barred," "out-to-get-her" competition.

Women like this come to work with the attitude that work is a cold, ugly war which only the tough will survive. Every woman is a potential enemy, a rival for the few slots at the top. These women don't pretend for a minute that cooperation is their goal. They compete by destroying, by making themselves look good at others' expense. If you've ever worked with someone like this, you know how uncomfortable it can be.

Marge is such a woman. She entered the corporate world reluctantly. She had wanted to earn a Ph.D. in comparative literature, but a divorce left her with three children and a determination to provide security for them and for her future. Marge saw the corporate world as a challenge and the women she worked with as obstacles to her advancement. Her intelligence and her ingratiating manner attracted attention from management, and she began on her road to success.

Always congenial with those who held the keys to the next door, Marge epitomizes to her female colleagues the type of woman who attacks with candy-coated claws. During a group meeting she cheerfully, smilingly, delivers vicious criticisms of her co-workers' performances. While assuring top management that she believes in developing cohesive teams, Marge manipulates the information she shares with her co-workers so no one in her group ever knows all that she knows. As a result, her co-workers can never catch up or compete with Marge on new proposals or projects. So far, the sheer strength of her ability has supported her promotions, but the women she manages and works with are beginning to draw together in resistance. The icy response she evokes in her female colleagues will soon crack the foundation of her rule. Her approach to competing by destroying others will eventually lead to her own destruction.

Another woman, Dawn, sees any successful woman in her electronics company as a potential rival, not only for her job but for attention and recognition from her male boss. Dawn prefers sabotage to criticism of competence as her method of operation. She works at corporate headquarters and is responsible for marketing support of new products. Georgia, a rising star for a mid-western division, requested that Dawn contact select representatives in the east and schedule a series of demonstrations and sales meetings for her product. Dawn's boss had mentioned Georgia's accomplishments and indicated to Dawn that Georgia was "one sharp woman."

A corporation can have only so many stars, according to Dawn, and she became determined that Georgia not be one of them. When Dawn's boss handed over a plum project for her to complete on a tight schedule, Dawn made an easy decision. She put her full effort into the project her boss gave her, and she neglected to follow through on Georgia's scheduling requests. When Georgia arrived in New York, ready for her sales meetings, she found no rooms had been scheduled, no equipment ordered, and no representatives invited. When she confronted Dawn, Dawn's response was to explain that her boss's project took priority and that Georgia should have checked back and handled the arrangements herself. Georgia didn't complain to Dawn's boss because she believed Dawn did have a good point about covering responsibilities herself and because complaining and bad-mouthing just weren't her style. Instead, Georgia explained the "miscommunication" to her division head and managed the arrangements for follow-up meetings herself. Before this incident, Georgia hadn't realized that Dawn saw her as a rival. But she learned. Never again will Georgia assume a woman is her friend until she has proven she can be trusted.

Those of us who believe women can be supporters, not rivals, have the responsibility to act on our values. Rivals destroy; supporters build the base for a secure future.

Once you identify a woman who sees you as a rival, you have to move carefully. Neither trust her nor court her. If you trust her, you can be sabotaged again. If you court her, she'll know she has you in a vulnerable position and that you're at her mercy! Do, however, acknowledge that she may well have information, experience, and influence that could benefit you—if you approach her with confidence in yourself and respect for the positions she holds.

Georgia now makes a point of asking Dawn for input early on when she undertakes a new project. This way Dawn experiences a sense of ownership and is less likely to undermine Georgia's plans. Also, Georgia tells me, "I have learned to never go to her city without making a point of stopping by to visit with her. In a way I'm paying my respects and Dawn appreciates this. Once, when I was late for an appointment and forgot to stop by, she was offended. She had let it be known through the grapevine that I had 'breezed in and out as if I owned the place.' That was my mistake! I respect that Dawn sees me as a rival, and I will be careful not to give her any further cause for complaints!"

Dealing with the Green-Eyed Monsters

No discussion of women and competition can be complete without a reference to the twin monsters, jealousy and envy. We become jealous when another woman wins a competition for a relationship with someone we value. We envy another woman who has position, power, or possessions we want for ourselves.

"Feelings of jealousy and envy are common with women," Barbara tells us. "It all comes back to the fundamental issues of self-esteem and self-worth. If a woman feels confident in her self-worth, she won't fear losing her identity if another woman performs better than she or threatens to gain advantage with a co-worker or superior. If she feels confident in her priorities and career decisions, she will be less likely to envy women in positions more desirable than her own."

More than 25 percent of the women answering our survey tell us that jealousy is a problem for women who work with women. However, during the process of interviewing over one hundred women for this book, not one woman wanted to discuss her feelings of jealousy and only a handful volunteered experiences with envy. "I understand their reluctance," Barbara explains. "In my office women often tell me, 'it's not that I'm jealous,' and then go on to describe their jealous feelings. We are taught jealousy isn't nice, so we deny being jealous."

Jealous behavior in defense of ourselves doesn't disappear as we move up in our organizations and careers. Though the competition may become more subtle, the barbs still draw blood. As Dr. Rosabeth Moss Kanter of the Harvard Business School said a few years ago in *Savvy*, "I notice that even in faculty meetings here, where we have three tenured women, there is subtle, unspoken pressure to be the first to put down the other women. It's a way of preserving your credibility."

Sometimes what women compete for is men. And when those women work together, expressions of jealousy can go beyond poison-tipped put-downs to intentional setups designed to destroy. I worked once at a school where two teachers had dated the same football coach. When he chose Maya over Joan, Joan burned with jealousy and planned revenge. She protested to the administration that Maya had unfairly graded students in a program they team-taught. She requested to be taken off the project so she could work with "credible professionals." And she totally fabricated a rumor that Maya had offered beer to students at a weekend cast party. Joan's jealousy won her no support, however, and eventually led to a year on probation when her attacks were discovered to be unfounded.

In situations like these, our responsibility to other women demands that we model control and not give in to our emotions. For too long women have damned each other and been damned by men for acting on our jealous feelings. Jealousy is an understandable response to competition; however, we have no excuse for punishing others for our losses or insecurities.

Jealousy has a sister named envy. Jealousy and envy often appear so much alike that it is hard to tell them apart. However, the women I talked with seemed to feel more comfortable discussing envy than jealousy. Jealousy strikes the vulnerable area of personal relationship; envy focuses its sights on what someone else possesses in position or material objects. Louise, a California business owner who has worked around the world, summarizes the difference between jealousy and envy this way: "It's okay to be envious. I can envy a woman who had the preparation and opportunity to work as a doctor in Nepal. I respect what she's doing and I would like to be doing something similar myself. But to be jealous of someone because she's a better friend of the ambassador than I am is negative. It says I'm small and bitter and don't have much pride in myself."

For those of us who work, surrounded by contemporaries and juniors moving ahead into positions with power and higher salaries than ours, a certain amount of envy is inevitable. During the eighties, didn't many of us envy (and despise) the superwoman who seemed to handle million-dollar accounts, tailored suits, international travel, and adorable children without getting a kink in her French braid?

We don't like being envious, but we can turn envy into a positive experience. If we exercise restraint and refuse to stoop to put-downs and sabotage when envy grips us, we can assess what the object of our envy has that we don't. And then we can ask ourselves what we need to do to get it for ourselves. Or, we may discover that what it takes to get the job, or the trip, or the car isn't worth what we're willing to give. "If we have healthy self-esteem," Barbara adds, "it's easier to manage an occasional bout of envy. When we feel good about who we are and what we're doing, we have less reason to envy someone else."

Kathy, a woman in her mid-thirties, was willing to discuss her experience with envy. Kathy enjoyed her job managing accounts for a Fortune 100 company. When a position opened up that would give her responsibility for an expanded list of major accounts, the challenge appealed to her. However, Kathy had a four-year-old and a baby at home, and she wondered whether she could handle the increased travel schedule and days away from her family. She decided not to apply for the position. "Actually," Kathy says looking back, "I just kind of let the deadline slip by."

When Kathy realized that Karen, a woman her own age who also had young children, had been selected for the position, Kathy was struck by a rush of envy that affected her like a fever. "Suddenly Karen had the opportunities I wanted," Kathy explains. "I saw her making more money and traveling on the company plane to meet customers from New York and London and Hong Kong. I wanted to see her exhausted and stressed. I wanted her to break down and snap at people during meetings. I wanted her to prove that my decision was right and that a woman can't have it all! But instead, she appeared exhilarated, and the company executives loved her work. She was away during the week but she had good child care and a helpful husband. She planned her weekends and had a wonderful time being a mom! I envied her, that's for sure, but I had no impulse to sabotage her successes. My problem was dealing with myself. When I was around her I felt disgusted, like my ambitions and career plans were all a sham. I felt I had let myself down, that I was a failure. I hated envying her, and I hated myself."

By the time I met Kathy, she had resolved her situation. The intense envy she felt toward Karen had helped her to put her own goals and priorities into perspective. She had decided that her preferences put being available to her family first, at least for the time being. She stopped considering herself a failure because she hadn't applied for the position. Instead, she became determined to observe and learn from her experience so that when the time was right, she would be ready to succeed with new challenges. Envy, for Kathy, led to self-awareness and a more secure self-esteem.

Competition among women sows the seeds for jealousy and envy. We may not be able to stop the feelings, but we can decide how we manage and express those feelings. Admitting that we are jealous and understanding why can be the first steps toward ending behaviors that disrupt the workplace and are unfair to other women. Some of us may choose to seek professional help in managing our jealousy and preparing ourselves to respond more professionally in a work context. Envy, on the other hand, can work to our own advantage if we take the opportunity to evaluate what we want and how we plan to accomplish our goals. In both cases, however, we must take the responsibility to move ourselves, and the women we work with, into a new climate where we control our emotions and focus on healthy relationships and productive work.

Becoming Comfortable with Competing

Competing might not be so difficult for women if we believed we were doing it "nicely." Recently I was interested to hear Maureen Farrow, a British cost construction analyst and company director, discussing on television what it takes for women to become successful. She conceded that to get to the top, women have had to compete. Then she added, "Hopefully, they have done it as nicely as possible."

For some of us, "competing nicely" or "nice competition" qualifies as an oxymoron. However, if we were to believe we were "being nice," perhaps many of us would have an easier time confronting competition and keeping relationship channels open at the same time.

We've all heard the argument that women have problems with competition because we didn't grow up playing team sports. Instead, we played take-turn games where we competed against ourselves. Boys, the story goes, learn to be aggressive and to want to win; girls, in contrast, learn to protect people's feelings and to abandon a game rather than threaten a relationship.

Where I grew up in the '50s, girls played team sports and they played to win. We competed, some more successfully than others, for spots on the hockey and basketball teams, and then for victories, playoffs, and titles. I have watched my son play soccer and football and have observed girls' volleyball, soccer, and basketball games. Everyone out there plays to win, but the teams function differently. The boys dispense with the niceties, to the other team and to each other, when someone misses a shot or a block. They yell what they think and then get back to playing the game.

The girls, on the other hand, spend a lot of time on and off the field consoling each other, encouraging each other, "being nice." At a girls' volleyball tournament the words "it's okay" ring off the walls as much as the balls off the net. The team members constantly assure each other that a mistake didn't break their connectedness. Though these girls are fierce competitors, they also take time to ask an opposing player if she's "okay" after a run-in or a fall. In other words, they find a balance between competition and connection, a balance that boys seem not to require and not to pursue.

Being nice makes women feel good and distracts us from the fact that we're competing (though many women, in sports particularly, say competing, playing hard, and wanting to win feels very good!). In the article, "But That's Not (Really) Mean: Competing in a Cooperative Mode," Linda A. Hughes discusses the way girls handle being both aggressive and nice. In her study of girls playing the game four-square, she observes that these young women adapt to competitive games where relationship conflicts could arise by being "nice-mean," covering the "mean" of getting someone out by the "nice" act of getting a friend in. Hughes uses her study to illustrate that cooperative social orientation is not "incompatible with competition among girls." Rather, "it shapes their way of competing."

Wanting to overshadow competition by being nice finds its way into many of our work environments. Wendy Bowers, a professional actress and film teacher, talks about the discomfort she and other women feel when competing and their need to do something "nice" to even the score. "I am a member of the Screen Actors Guild in Los Angeles, and so is my husband," she tells me. "The competition in L.A. is tough. Only 20 percent of the work goes to women. The majority of the actresses avoid each other. We're always thinking, 'Is she getting what I want?' In an audition room full of men, the atmosphere, my husband tells me, is relaxed. They know what everyone wants and what they're up against. The men are prepared to accept winning or losing, and they can walk away feeling okay.

"But oh, the situation is a bit different for the women! We're uncomfortable with the blatant competition, and the tension in an audition room is palpable. The level of fear is something I can't quite express. Women are afraid of losing. The level of want is high. Then the auditions are over and everyone goes home. But the women can't just walk away. We feel responsible for the other women, especially if we win. We worry, 'I should give her a call, see if she's okay.' Women feel responsible for taking care of each other, even when we're competing for our jobs, for our lives!"

We can learn to be nice when we compete. Being nice means playing fair, respecting those we are competing with, and caring that each of us has a chance to express our best. Women's team sports can serve as a model for the workplace. Each member has worked hard to earn her place on the team, and each one strives to contribute the winning shot. We support our stars who, in turn, know that winning as a team depends on everyone contributing her skills and effort. We express our caring with coaching, and with extra support when someone strikes out or drops the ball. When we find ourselves in competitive situations, we have a model. And yes, for those of us who hope we will compete "nicely," we will.

Competing with Ourselves

When I first began talking with women about how they competed, I dismissed women who said "I have never competed with another woman" as out of touch. I assumed they were evading an unpleasant reality, and I categorized their approach to competition as denial. I've since come to appreciate that these women are telling the truth and demonstrate one model of how we can all successfully approach competition in the future.

Joanna works for a company that uses comparative ratings to determine salaries. "I never think about competing when I'm working with women and men on my team," she tells me. "I feel comfortable in a cooperative environment. Ratings and evaluations are the furthest things from my mind when we're into a project. I just want to perform well and support the effort. I take pride in being able to contribute valuable input and follow-through. If I stopped for a minute to consider that I was competing with these people, the sense of teamwork and cooperation would be lost. It's the spirit of cooperation that makes my job rewarding. Maybe we're competing in a sense, but we're cooperating too. Cooperation is where I keep my focus."

Joanna challenges herself to excellent performance and maintains a cooperative attitude. She knows that her performance will be compared to others' at her level, but she doesn't see herself as competing with anyone but herself.

A woman I mentioned earlier, Jacqueline, is now co-director in program administration for ETS in Princeton, New Jersey. Jacqueline has been a program administrator in the public schools, and she was a funded researcher before beginning her career at ETS. Yet when I asked her to talk about her experiences competing with other women, she claimed she had never competed. When I asked her to explain how she had gotten her job with the school district and her promotions at ETS, she stated flatly that she had been offered the positions because she was the best candidate. "But weren't you competing?" I asked. "Not against anyone," she told me. "I was presenting my credentials and my record and hoping they would offer me the job based on what they saw."

Jacqueline maintains a professional and friendly relationship with her co-director. When they both apply for the director's position, Jacqueline will again present her credentials—not to compete against another woman, but to look forward to new challenges and new opportunities.

Competing with ourselves, rather than against other women, encourages us to continue our achievements while acknowledging that other women will be challenging themselves as well. Kristen, a graduate of Boston College and, at twenty-seven, a manager for Andersen Consulting in Boston, in retrospect realizes she could have developed a competitive rivalry with Aimee, a young woman from Brown University who joined Andersen when Kristen did. Instead, Kristen welcomed Aimee as a bright, dedicated co-worker who challenged her to keep learning and keep improving her best performance. "In a sense," Kristen says, "I'm using Aimee in a positive way to motivate and check myself on how well I am doing."

In *Secrets Between Us: Women and Competition*, Laura Tracy talks about a new generation of women who know that "when you care, you compete. That way, each woman enhances her own development while challenging another woman's growth." Women who compete with this understanding of challenge and personal growth give us the models we need for a positive, powerful future.

Kathy Canclini, a nurse-educator with a large urban hospital, acknowledges she is competing with another administrator but sees the competition as a way to make "good women even better." Kathy knows both she and Marla want to move up to the same position; however, instead of hiding her ambitions or maneuvering to discredit Marla, Kathy has chosen to observe Marla's strengths and to learn from them. "Marla handles some management tasks better than I do," Kathy says. "She's very organized and assertive. I consciously watch what she does and try to incorporate her strengths into my style. She appreciates how I work with people and bring staff teams together. We maintain a professional distance, but we respect each other's abilities. Whichever one of us gets the promotion this time will have the other's support. We learn from each other and we'll be better when our turn comes."

A goal when women compete, whether with ourselves or openly with others, is to maintain a supportive and cooperative environment. Women in companies such as Hewlett-Packard and Levi Strauss are forming support groups: women from one department or women from a variety of departments and functional levels come together informally to talk about themselves and share information about their organizations. In this setting, women talk openly about their ambitions. They ask for and receive help writing resumes and preparing for interviews. When one woman gets the promotion she wanted, the group feels vested in the accomplishment. A woman who moves ahead acknowledges the women who have helped her and shares what she is learning with the group. She has a support system in place on which to build not only her future, but the future of all women.

Competition can become a comfort zone for women in the future. First, though, we must accept that competition need not mean winning while another loses, or fighting to defeat a rival. Competition for competition's sake probably will never be acceptable to most women. We value our relationships and will resist a hostile, competitive environment that threatens the strength and benefits we gain when we cooperate. Instead, we can reconsider how competition can function when women lead in the workplace. Healthy competition for women will focus on each one of us challenging ourselves to keep growing and keep going.

Positive competition for women will take place in a cooperative context. We will learn to become comfortable talking about opportunities that exist for all of us and being open about our career goals. We will welcome women who acknowledge they have ambitions, valuing the challenge they offer us to keep improving ourselves. And we will support women who show us how far we can go and what we can achieve. Women working together, cooperating and competing in a mutual effort to be our best, create a unified power base for advancing our strengths into the 21st century.

Suggestions for Comfortable Competition

* If you find yourself competing with a co-worker for an opportunity or promotion, accept that competition is a necessary reality in the workplace. Don't withdraw from competing, or deny you are competing, because you experience competition with women as uncomfortable. Understand that you are competing with yourself to be your best, not to defeat someone else.

* Consider letting other women know when you have decided to pursue an opportunity. Publicly acknowledging when we are applying for a promotion may discourage "behind-the-back" sabotage by women whose motives in bad-mouthing others would be immediately suspect. Letting others know when we decide to pursue a promotion lets us, and the women we work with, prepare for a positive continuity of support as we achieve our advancements.

* Invite other women into the competitive situation. Ask Jane to write you a recommendation or help you prepare for an interview. In this way, your co-workers can learn from your experience and share in your success. When we contribute to another woman's achievements, we are helping each other be our best together.

7

The Friendship Dilemma

No issue comes closer to the emotional quick for women who work together than the conflict between friendship demands and workplace realities. This conflict is a uniquely female dilemma. We have brought with us to work an expectation for the caring, supportive, affectionate friendships we have enjoyed as girls and as women in our neighborhoods and communities.

But the workplace is different. Our jobs demand that we respect the realities of doing business and surviving in our careers, and often workplace demands conflict with friendship expectations. Women are asked to choose between honoring first their friendship or their work. The choices can be painful either way, and for all people involved.

How we approach the friendship dilemma relates to our personal values and our understanding of the risks and consequences involved in trying to balance friendship needs and workplace demands. For some of us, the value of an intimate relationship with a nurturing friend overshadows the risks of establishing such a relationship with a co-worker. For all of us, to confront the friendship dilemma with maturity means we must know ourselves, know the risks, and manage our personal boundaries in respect to ourselves and the women we would choose as our friends.

For many of us, today's workplace is our entire community, our neighborhood. The work site provides health and social services, recreational activities, and opportunities to become involved with people far beyond our job functions. We laugh at work, we cry, we reach out to and need each other. We transfer to a new location and the people at work become our resource for everything from where to shop to how to arrange a funeral. After commuting, working eight to twelve hours, and coming home to take care of our families, many of us have little time to pursue friendships beyond work. So we naturally gravitate toward being friends with the women with whom we work.

Both our desire for friendships at work and the problems inherent in those friendships came up over and over again in our survey. One-third of the respondents said they like working with women because "women form friendships." They told us they like the camaraderie of women, the "closer relationships," the "trust and trusting" that takes place on a personal level. However, an almost equal number of women identified "betrayal" as a significant negative characteristic in women-working-with-women relationships. They said repeatedly that women are "two-faced," and "willing to play friend, then knife you in the back."

During interviews, I heard again and again stories of how friendships threaten the proper function of office communications. Women tell us that friendships make it difficult to criticize co-workers or to make decisions that go against what a friend wants and expects. Friendships also make it difficult for us to distance ourselves from personal situations, even when our work responsibilities demand that we do so.

When I first read Tara Roth Madden's indictment of female friendships at work, *Women vs Women: The Uncivil Business War*, I felt she was being harsh and absolute. "Female office friendships can become as complicated as office romances, " she writes. "They interfere with business and interfere with business decorum. They place restrictions on the strictly business aspects of advancing up the professional ladder. Contradictory expectations fuel the flames."

I objected to Madden's attack on anything as sacred as the bond of intimate friendship between women. However, after interviewing many women from corporations, professional settings, and small partnerships, I have re-evaluated my initial response. Today I am convinced women must heed Madden's warning and the warnings of other women who have found the conflicts between friendship and work more than they could manage.

Learning to communicate with each other about the implications of friendship at work may help us to avoid the confusion, hurt, and betrayal that seem particularly painful when practical work priorities put friendship second. Being aware is being prepared. If we know the potential pitfalls, we have the option of being careful with intense friendships at work: ending ones we need to end, or taking the chance with ones that promise great value for us.

We can also choose to recognize and develop a new form of relationships, work friendships. Work friendships let us acknowledge our affinity for certain women we meet on the job, but they don't carry the expectations of a traditional full-blown friendship. In work friendships lies the answer to how women can balance our affection and appreciation for other women with our responsibility to workplace demands.

What Do We Mean by Friendship?

Men and women define friendship differently. "In the White Male System," psychotherapist Anne Wilson Schaef argues, "a friend is someone who can be relied upon to support the 'team effort.' A friend is a 'buddy,' a 'pal.' In the Female System, friendship involves basic respect, trust, and knowing and being known." For women, she continues, "the focus of friendship is verbal intimacy and mutual sharing of one's being. True friends are those who totally expose themselves to each other, sure in the knowledge that to do so is *safe*."

Safety is the issue here. As Schaef notes, women's friendships tend to be more intense and affectionate than men's. Men focus their friendships around activities, what they are doing together, while women use talk to bring them closer together. We use talk to build trust. We want to believe that sharing is safe and that our friends will respect our trust. Men find "buddies" at work and extend the tasks they share on the job to other activities, which may include golf afternoons, ball games, poker matches, or bike trips. As activities shift, so can the buddies involved.

Men's ability to be involved with one another without being intimate allows them to compete without the discomfort female relationships can engender. Men seem better prepared than women to see each other as functioning entities within the work context; they can more easily shift their friendships to suit their job alignment. Women, on the other hand, can suffer pangs of guilt or experience residual hurt when job demands conflict with friendship expectations.

Rita had made friends with Lyn, her manager, when Rita first moved to Cincinnati. They worked well together and, both being young and single, extended their relationship to weekend movies, shopping, and watching videos at each other's apartments. They came to rely on each other for fun and for emotional support when times got tough. When Rita applied for and received a transfer and a promotion, Lyn was deeply hurt while Rita felt guilty and responsible for "breaking up their friendship."

"Before I left," Rita says, "Lyn called me into her office. She said she had learned a lesson and wanted to share it with me. 'Never,' she told me, 'let a work relationship become a friendship.' She said that my leaving hurt her and that she would miss me. She believed we could not continue the friendship once I had requested to transfer and could now be competing with her. Then she said, 'I'll never again make a friend at work. I may be lonely, but work will be easier that way.'"

Though Rita realizes that all friendships face loss when one of the friends moves away or circumstances change, she also realizes that the work connection made her decision to leave more poignant and more absolute. She understands how putting her career goals first hurt Lyn, and she will not inflict that experience on other women she meets. If she does find herself attracted to the possibility of friendship with a co-worker, she now will talk with that person about how their career priorities may affect their friendship in the future. If they both understand the conflicts they may face, communicating about those challenges may allow them to achieve a balance of risks each can accept.

Lyn had personalized her relationship with Rita beyond a practical workplace relationship. The two shared a friendship that was emotionally grounded more in their personal lives than their work connections. For Lyn, separating from Rita meant more than facing adjustment to a new co-worker. It meant readjusting her personal life, her emotional support structure, and her way of living.

"Women need intimacy and sharing of their personal selves," Barbara comments. "Like Lyn, many women face loneliness outside their work environment. So they turn to the women they see every day and seek friendship in those relationships. When the job situations shift, these women can be left feeling hurt and empty. They blame their friends for putting work first without considering that perhaps their friends really had no choice. I wish I could say we do, but women today don't always have the luxury of putting our friendships first when our job opportunities, our survival, is on the line."

A Friendship Quiz

To bring the problems inherent in friendships at work into focus for you, I have drawn up a list of statements you can answer either "yes" or "no." Please consider each situation and give your gut-level, heart-felt response. (We all may know the most appropriate answers, but what motivates us at work can often be what we feel rather than what we know.)

If you have a friend at work, would you:

1. Feel uncomfortable criticizing her actions/attitudes?

2. Give special consideration to her when opportunities or promotions are available?

3. Talk with her openly and honestly about your fears, weaknesses, or worries?

4. Feel uncomfortable competing with her for opportunities or promotions?

5. Let what you know of her through social or family interactions affect your attitude toward her at work?

6. Feel hurt if she criticized your work-related performance?

7. Feel betrayed if she used an intimacy you shared to deny you an opportunity or promotion?

8. Feel abandoned if she accepted a promotion in another city?

9. Resent her pursuing opportunities that would improve her work status over yours?

10. Expect her to give priority to resolving personal issues between the two of you before focusing on work?

Our answers to these friendship issues give us insight into our personal friendship requirements. When we answer "yes" to any of these questions, we must understand that our expectations can potentially impede workplace productivity and performance or leave our friends at work feeling angry and betrayed.

Betrayal

When we identify another woman as our friend, we trust her to respect our secrets and celebrate in our good fortune. We let our guard down and don't exercise the same caution in sharing information we might with our other co-workers. This can sometimes lead to betrayal, or at least a sense of betrayal, by one of our work-friends.

Tonya supervised a workroom of women who prepared test results on scientific instruments. Beth Ann, Tonya's friend, supervised a similar group in another area. When their company decided to expand, they created a new supervisory position to oversee all testing rooms. Tonya's manager told her she had been selected for the job but asked her not to tell anyone yet as the company wanted to announce the position and accept applications. Tonya, naturally excited, went straight to Beth Ann to tell her the good news. Beth Ann responded coolly at first, and Tonya blamed herself for not considering Beth Ann's feelings. The next day Beth Ann went to the company president threatening to file a complaint that offering Tonya the job without announcing it first was unfair.

Tonya was stunned that her friend would take her secret and challenge her in such a public way. Tonya told our workshop group that she felt "gouged and betrayed." She had thought Beth Ann could be trusted as a true friend; she learned that where promotions and a higher salary are at stake, friendship rules can quickly go out the window.

Beth Ann's behavior may seem extreme and you may rightly ask what kind of a true friend would ever behave like that. However, this is a true story, one that I heard repeated in different forms by many women. Tonya did not know until she trusted Beth Ann with her news that Beth Ann would respond the way she did. In the future, Tonya has the option of discussing potential conflicts early in a relationship or protecting herself, and her friend as well, by not testing the relationship with work-related confidences.

Mary is another woman who learned the hard way that sharing good fortune with a friend invites betrayal when salary and opportunity are on the line. Mary worked as an independent CPA and heard of an opening with one of the best accounting firms in town. Excited, she called her friend Margo and asked if they could meet to work on Mary's resume and interview skills. They had helped each other in the past, and Mary thought, "Who better to support me now than Margo!"

Margo, also a CPA, had not heard of the job opening until Mary told her; right after the phone conversation, she called the firm and requested an interview, which they scheduled for the next day. Of course, when Mary heard how Margo had treated her confidence, she became deeply upset and felt betrayed by her "best friend."

After I told Tonya's and Mary's stories during one workshop, an attractive woman raised her hand to interject a comment. She introduced herself as a visitor from Norway where she held a government position overseeing county health administrations. She was the only female at her level of government service. She said she could not believe Tonya's story or the other betrayal stories she was hearing. "I would never, never," she said, "share any information that would let another woman gain advantage on me. It just makes good common sense. Unless I wanted to share the opportunity with her, I would never put her in a position where she would have to choose between me as her friend and a job she might have. In Norway, we keep our friendships and our work relationships separate to protect ourselves and each other from just the situations you describe." Perhaps we can learn from our Norwegian colleagues.

If Mary had anticipated a conflict with Margo, she might not have so willingly shared the information about the CPA position. Perhaps only after being offered the job should she have shared the good news with Margo. She could then explain why, to protect their friendship, she had not put herself and Margo in the difficult position of competing against each other for the same job. As friends, they could talk about their career needs and the importance of their friendship.

Such communication between women may be sensitive, but it is necessary if we are to keep both our friendships and careers functioning. I am reminded here of Sheryl, an executive secretary who honored friendship over her job and ended up losing both! Had she been able to talk about her friendship expectations with her friend Alexis, she might have avoided a painful end to a friend/work conflict.

Sheryl met Alexis, an account auditor, during a quality training program for their company. They enjoyed uproarious sessions over coffee and cheesecake where they reviewed their daily lives and scrutinized office politics. In the course of one conversation, Alexis told Sheryl about a rumor she had heard that a longtime product was to be phased out. This came as quite a shock to Sheryl, whose boss would be directly affected. Feeling obligated to warn him, Sheryl told her boss the rumor on the following day. He demanded to know the source of the rumor, and when Sheryl refused, he threatened to fire her for insubordination. Sheryl stood by her belief that you don't snitch on your friend, and her boss made good on his promise.

Sheryl believed Alexis would appreciate the protection, and Alexis did thank her for not revealing her identity. However, Alexis offered no condolences or help for Sheryl in finding a new job. The friendship became strained and Sheryl grew to resent her loss. "I feel betrayed," she told Barbara later in a counseling session. "I honored the friendship and ended up with nothing—no job and no friend."

Expectations we have about friendships and friendship behaviors often conflict with who we need to be and how we should act in our careers. If we can't talk through these conflicts with work-friends, we have the responsibility to at least protect ourselves and the women we care about by not sharing information a friend could use to our disadvantage.

Whether in the community or at work, there are levels of friendship and levels of confidence. We need to choose our levels of intimacy based on our circumstances and, of course, on how well we communicate with and trust our friend. Our choice may be to hold back, and not be absolutely open and trusting. This decision may not be wholly satisfying, but the control we gain over our relationship and the situation may mean less pain, both for ourselves and for our friends. No one can betray us if we have disclosed nothing we wish to keep confidential.

Competition

The difficulty of competing with friends for career advancement and opportunities was discussed in Chapter Six. In some cases, though, the competition focuses not on which friend will win the prize but on friendship itself as the prize. Women often compete with one another for friendship, and the workplace does not protect us from jealous women who resent our relationships with other co-workers. Unfortunately, women who act out this jealousy act up difficult hurdles for all of us to navigate.

Irene faced such a hurdle when Pat pitted herself against Irene for Marcia's allegiance. Irene and Pat were assigned as project leaders to what Pat perceived to be rival teams. Marcia and Irene had been good friends for a while; but now that Marcia was on Pat's team, Pat saw Marcia's relationship with Irene as a threat to her authority. "Pat's team was Pat's territory," Irene reports. "If I so much as stopped to talk with Marcia at her desk or walked to the parking lot with her, Pat's claws came out. She so much as told me to stay away from Marcia. Marcia was hers. Essentially she felt her authority was threatened by Marcia's friendship with me and she was not subtle in trying to control our relationship. It didn't matter if we were talking about where to buy purple petunias. Any contact was perceived by Pat as a challenge to her authority and to her team function."

Irene's concern was that Marcia, being in a subordinate position to Pat, would ultimately bear the bruises of this territorial battle. Irene decided that no contact with Marcia at work was her best choice to reduce workplace tensions and to get herself focused back on her job. However, Irene and Marcia had become so conscious about their relationship that they even felt uncomfortable with their evening phone calls or early morning meetings at the bagel shop. Inadvertently, their friendship had created conflicts between both work teams and a competition for what Pat saw as "control" over Marcia. Luckily, Irene and Marcia were able to talk about the problem. They decided together it would be easier for everyone if they put their relationship on hold for the duration of Pat's project.

In another instance, Darcy didn't anticipate Julia's competitiveness nor her jealousy. New to the office and in need of a friend, Darcy welcomed Julia's overtures of friendship. They walked to the parking lot together and talked on the phone about their personal lives, their plans for the future, and their past relationships. With the intimacy of friendship, Julia came to expect an exclusiveness between them. Darcy, on the other hand, was naturally outgoing, and she adjusted quickly to the new office. When she began a friendly relationship with Jeff, the branch manager, Julia became jealous and backed off from her friendship with Darcy.

Darcy was busy meeting new people and didn't realize anything was wrong until she noticed Julia spending every free minute with Annie, a new transfer. Darcy supervised Annie, and during their first performance review Annie attacked Darcy for being a poor manager. She claimed Darcy had not given her adequate feedback or enough responsibility. "I heard Julia's voice in Annie's accusations," Darcy says, "and I knew this was Julia's way of punishing me for becoming friends with Jeff. She had set Annie up to get back at me. When I asked Annie what responsibilities she wanted or what feedback she needed, she drew a blank. I asked her directly if Julia had coached her before the review and she admitted Julia had not only told Annie what to say but had also prepared Annie to distrust anything positive I might say! Honestly, I never imagined that acting like friends with someone at work could lead to such a mess. I've learned, though. From now on I'll stay friendly with everyone, but become exclusive with no one!"

Julia's response may seem extreme for some of us who believe we left such behaviors behind us in junior high school. However, this story is similar to many stories I've heard from other women, and it tells me we should all be prepared for jealousy if we form exclusive friendships at work. It's unfortunate that women competing for friendships can exhibit such unpleasant and unproductive behavior. Darcy's resolution to stay friendly but not become intimate with anyone at work underlines an alternative all women should consider to preserve good working relationships.

Exclusive Friendships

Even happy, close friendships can put serious kinks in the communication flow necessary to keep a workplace running smoothly and productively. Indeed, exclusive friendships can make it difficult for co-workers to work around the relationship or for others to know how to intrude when work needs to get done. Often, women who become intent on their friendship don't realize the impact their exclusivity has on workplace operations. Once they do, however, they have the option to keep a professional distance at work while saving the friendship for after work.

Deana came to me for help with her resume. She had decided to leave her job with a national toy franchise because of an "impossible situation" with two women, Joan and Peggy, who let their friendship distract them from their responsibilities managing retail operations. Joan and Peggy had previously both been assistant managers in different departments, but now Peggy had been promoted and the two of them spent most of their time together, often in Peggy's office, talking and laughing. Other workers in the store felt uncomfortable interrupting their "gab sessions" with questions or feedback on operations.

Communication became especially difficult when the supervisors under Joan, Deana among them, felt Joan was "letting the department go" by not keeping up with inventory or listening to problems the salespeople were having. They believed they couldn't complain to the manager, Peggy, because when they tried, Peggy dismissed the complaints with some comment about how tired Joan had been and how they all needed to be "less bitchy."

"We've talked about this among ourselves," Deana told me. "We feel their friendship has taken over their responsibilities to the store. They seem to care more about their relationship than running the store. We can't complain, because they either won't hear us or they defend each other! The situation is impossible!"

Two months later, I ran into Deana. She told me that the national corporation was closing the store for which she, Joan, and Peggy had worked. The operation had been poorly managed and the building was for sale. Deana speculated that the kink Joan and Peggy's friendship put in the communication flow had contributed significantly to the store's demise. If Joan and Peggy had been able to detach from their friendship long enough to consider how their attentions to each other were compromising store operations, Deana and the others might still have their jobs.

What Joan and Peggy didn't learn, however, Deana did. She will talk about friendship and work priorities first whenever she feels drawn toward an exclusive work relationship. "I appreciate friendship," she says, "but when I take a job, I respect what the job demands. And I expect any woman who would be my friend would respect those priorities too."

Anticipating conflicts between friendship and work and talking about them with our friends can prepare us to communicate openly when we face a challenge to our friendship. "I wish," Corrina told me after reading an early draft of this chapter, "that Stephanie and I had talked about our work styles earlier. I value my intimate friendship with Stephanie and I don't want to risk losing what we share. But now she is going through a relationship crisis in her personal life and she needs to talk. Every time she has a few minutes, she stops by my cubical and wants me to stop what I'm doing and listen. I have never made it clear that when I have a deadline, my style is to push straight ahead. I don't handle interruptions well because they distract my attention. However, I am in a bind because I don't want to risk offending Stephanie and compromising the trusting relationship we share."

Corrina realized she faced a problem in her friendship with Stephanie and she weighed the risks and consequences. She could not stay constantly available to Stephanie and maintain her performance on tight project deadlines. The friendship was extremely valuable to Corrina—but so was her job.

Finally, Corrina decided to talk with Stephanie directly about the conflict she was experiencing. She made it clear that their friendship mattered tremendously and that she would feel more comfortable with their relationship if they could accept each other's styles and work/friendship needs. Stephanie understood completely and thanked Corinna for her honesty and caring. By taking the risk of communicating, Corinna's action led to a positive resolution of a work versus friendship dilemma. Both she and Stephanie value what they have learned. They make a point of talking openly with other women about the risks we face when we choose to pursue friendships and about the value of healthy communication in preparing us to face and resolve our challenges.

Criticizing Friends

Understandably, friends don't want to criticize their friends. Perhaps we don't recognize performance problems when we concentrate on the qualities that we admire in our friends; perhaps we don't want to hurt our friends' feelings by identifying their faults. Ideally, a true friend will accept, even welcome, constructive criticism as a sign of caring and kind concern. However, in a work situation, a manager who has to give a negative performance evaluation to a friend finds herself in a one-up, judgmental position. Many of us feel uncomfortable in such positions, and some of us respond by avoiding or overlooking problems.

That is what Rea, a manager, had done with her friend Suzy, and the problems fell to Sabina when she took over Rea's position. Sabina's department works on a compensation budget where employees are paid for performance. Shortly after taking over for Rea, Sabina discovered that Suzy's performance fell considerably below standard though she was paid for above average work. Sabina worried that Suzy would be "crushed, destroyed" when Sabina confronted her with her negative evaluation. When Sabina did present Suzy with her poor evaluation and, in fact, put her on probation for inadequate performance, Suzy was crushed. She had no idea her work had been inferior. Her friend, Rea, had never given her anything but encouragement!

The friendship between Rea and Suzy had made necessary communication on performance impossible for Rea. As a result, Sabina inherited a "poorly managed" department, one major problem being that Suzy wasn't doing her job. Rea's protective impulse not only hurt the department but also denied Suzy the constructive feedback she needed to improve her job performance. Finally, it set Suzy up for a devastating confrontation with reality, to say nothing of the possibility that she could lose her job.

Honest, direct communication on the sensitive issue of criticism may seem very threatening to some women, but it could have saved Suzy, and Sabina, some painful moments. If women can manage kind, caring criticism as part of their friendships, their relationships may survive in the workplace. If not, they can choose to depersonalize their friendships and establish more professional relationships. In the end, we all need to realize that when friendship prohibits necessary communication or truthful criticism, seldom does anyone benefit.

Favoring Friends

Most of us learned as young girls that friends help their friends. Friends have a special relationship. We serve as advocates for one another. We "pull" for our friends and expect similar favors in return. Because our female friendships affect us deeply on a personal level, the expectation that friends should favor one another presents agonizing challenges for some women with friends in the workplace.

The difficulty of making a decision affecting a friend tortured Lois for two weeks before she acted on her business priorities. Lois went to Barbara when she first realized she had to choose between the best for her business or the best for her friend.

Lois worked for an employee-vested realty company as office manager. Karen moved to town with her six-year-old son following an acrimonious divorce. Lois and Karen met at a school carnival and liked each other immediately. Karen asked Lois about job situations, and Lois suggested she apply at the realty company as a secretary-receptionist. The president hired her, and the two women, who now saw each other every day, pursued their friendship. Since both were single with young boys, they spent weekends together watching soccer or meeting for pizza. They shared their life experiences, education plans, fears, and frustrations. Karen openly admitted to disliking intensely one of the realty partners who reminded her of her ex. She confided that she panicked under too much stress and would simply "let things go" rather than try to manage her time. Over coffee, Karen would laughingly tell Lois about the realtors' reaction to "mess ups" on messages or misplaced contract information.

Karen was delighted to have found a friend like Lois; Lois welcomed the friendship as well—that is, until the company decided to open a branch east of town and asked Lois to select the new office manager. Lois' job security depended on the realty company prospering. She had to make the best decision for the business, but she also had an obligation to her friend. Karen knew about the expansion and talked comfortably with Lois about how much fun it would be when they each had their own office to manage. Karen assumed that Lois would select her for the position. After all, they were best friends and Lois knew how much Karen could use the salary increase!

Lois, however, questioned seriously what to do. In good faith, she could not trust operation of the new office to Karen, who had neither the temperament nor the skills to manage the position. Lois decided to select someone with more experience, better skills, and demonstrated responsibility. When Lois personally told Karen of her hiring decision, something Lois felt she had to do in respect to their friendship, Karen was shocked at first and then became furiously angry. "How could you, how could you?" Karen repeated over and over again. "I was your best friend! How could you do this to me!"

When Lois tried to explain that she still cared for Karen, Karen called her a liar and ran from the office. For the next two weeks, before she moved away to live with her parents, Karen spread the word all over town that Lois was a deceptive liar who had led Karen to believe she was her friend when, in fact, she betrayed the friendship. Though Barbara assured Lois that she had made the appropriate decision, Lois still felt that in some way she had betrayed a friendship trust.

"I should have anticipated the situation," Lois reflected after talking with Barbara. "I would have been a better friend if I had let Karen know when she started telling me how she functioned at work that she was headed for problems. I should have said directly that I might someday have to make a work decision based on her performance. I could have suggested stress management courses. Maybe our friendship would have changed, but I could have helped to prevent all the hurt and anger she feels."

The pressure Lois felt when she had to make a business decision affecting her friend came from the expectations she believed Karen had for their friendship. In another case, Phyllis felt a similar pressure from her friend Janell, but even more so from other women in the department who were watching her. For Phyllis, the expectations of others made making a decision affecting Janell a "damned if I do, damned if I don't" situation.

Phyllis had advanced quickly into a first-level management position with a large insurance company. When Janell joined the company as a trainee, Phyllis recognized her strong abilities and made an extra effort to offer Janell advice and opportunity. The two women were both in their twenties and they shared interests from country swing to turtle cheesecakes. A natural affinity for one another led to a mutually appreciative friendship. They didn't consider their relative positions at work as important, until Phyllis had a job to fill that would mean a promotion for Janell. Phyllis knew Janell was well qualified and, based on all objective criteria, should get the promotion. But everyone knew the two women were friends. If Phyllis promoted Janell over the other trainees, the other women in the office would assume it was because of their friendship; both women would be subjecting themselves to resentment and even hostility.

If Phyllis didn't promote Janell, however, Janell would certainly wonder why her friend had selected someone else. And even if Phyllis had good reasons for not promoting Janell, the other women could interpret Phyllis's decision as a breach of friendship. They would then question Phyllis's ability to stand solid and treat the rest of them fairly!

Phyllis did decide to promote Janell, and she did listen to complaints of favoritism. Phyllis realized that maintaining their friendship in the office context was going to continue creating challenges for both her and Janell. So she initiated a conversation with Janell that directly addressed these issues. Out of respect for the work environment and their career potentials, Phyllis and Janell agreed to lessen their non-work-related friendship. When they did get together for music or dessert, they invited other people from work to join them. Inviting other women into their relationship countered the impression of exclusivity and led to a more comfortable office environment in which they could function as friendly co-workers and not as obligated friends.

Doing Business as Friends

Women who go into business together often find themselves in friendship situations before they realize what has happened. If we aren't careful, such friendships can intrude on our business responsibilities and compromise our focus and productivity.

Barbara and I had known each other casually before becoming involved together with WomenWorks. We lived in the same neighborhood and had sons the same age who were friends. But we hadn't become involved in each other's lives until we began working together.

We started walking together in the mornings, and soon we were sharing histories and feelings on a very personal level. Our relationship developed the emotional context so much a part of female friendships. Barbara learned that I battle many insecurities and that I can't be as detached as I would like from the emotional ups and downs in my children's lives. I learned about Barbara's conflicts with people in her family and within the community. I knew how offended and hurt she could be by seemingly innocent interactions, be they holiday invitations or family events. We became sensitive to each other's state of feeling. When one of us was off balance, the other felt drawn to help her back to equilibrium.

Soon Barbara and I began planning weekend activities together with our families and enjoyed water skiing days and oldies rock concerts. The phone rang at all hours to "just check up" or share some good news. Our WomenWorks planning meetings were up-beat gatherings of the two of us with Betty, who contributed good ideas and energy but maintained a pleasant professional distance.

Then, all of a sudden, the friendship cooled between our sons. As mothers, we each sided with our own sons in the conflict; as friends, we empathized with each other's feelings. The tensions were palpable at the next WomenWorks meeting. Barbara knew how vulnerable I could be to my children's mistakes, and I knew how emotionally Barbara could respond to a perceived wrong. We couldn't give our full attention to important decisions. Every issue that came up at our meeting tapped an emotional chord and alerted our defenses. We managed a surface decorum, but we were seriously distracted and unable to detach ourselves enough from the situation to give our business the priority it deserved.

After two such sessions, with our attentions focused more on feelings than finances, Barbara and I realized we had to confront the issue. Our personal relationship was eclipsing our business relationship; we had to get back to a more professional base. We understood that the only way to do this was to stop interacting with each other as social friends, to stop exposing our vulnerabilities and bringing our expectations for emotional involvement into work.

Barbara and I never sat down and talked through our friendship/business conflict. The situation was obvious to both of us, and we backed off silently from the daily intimacy of our friendship. To protect WomenWorks and ourselves, we stopped walking in the mornings and telephoning without a work-connected reason. We no longer planned weekend activities together. Still, we remain friendly and enjoy catching up on the whos and whats of each other's lives when we meet in the neighborhood or have time before a WomenWorks meeting begins. Otherwise, at work we concentrate on business. Today our business relationship succeeds because we respect the limits the work environment places on friendship, and we keep our attention on our professional futures.

In *Women vs Women: The Uncivil Business War*, Madden suggests that women like Barbara and me, who find ourselves involved in friendships at work, should initiate a "trial separation" thus ending the relationship immediately. Her "cold turkey" approach instructs women to stop "all lunches, personal calls, coffee breaks, after-hours socializing, and office confidences about anything other than business." Ending a friendship that started at work can be painful for everyone. But when friends can talk about the reasons for ending the friendship, it can be understood as an act of kindness, an expression of true caring for each other's opportunities and future.

When Friends Go Into Business Together

The friendship between Barbara and me grew once we had entered a business arrangement with each other. In other situations, women who are already friends agree to extend that friendship into a business partnership. When women do this, they often have to choose between continuing their friendship, continuing the business, or establishing a conscious, negotiated middle ground.

Three women I know became friends when their children attended the same elementary school. Rather than look for work when their youngest children started school, they decided to start a retail business selling educational materials for schools and parents.

As friends, Jean had been the strong one; she was always there with a cool head and a warm laugh. Trixie liked to protect her independence, yet she joined her friends in sharing deeply personal feelings about her need for a "life of her own." Diana was an extremely sensitive and introspective person, and she had been the most needful of emotional support.

It was Trixie who had suggested the idea of starting the business. She knew that Jean had been a business major and had worked in retail before starting her family. As the non-business majors of the group, Trixie and Diana signed up for a small business ownership course at the community college. After drawing up a business plan and finding a willing bank, the friends were in business. Soon, however, it became apparent that the women had incompatible notions of what the business meant. Jean saw the company as her future and she expended effort commensurate with her goals. Trixie enjoyed the challenge and worked hard, but she didn't want to continue with the store forever. Diana, who didn't really need to make money, liked seeing her friends on the days she was scheduled to work; but clearly the store was not her highest priority.

After less than a year, Jean decided she could no longer work with Diana. The dependence that had created a base for a caring and sharing friendship conflicted with the need for all business partners to have strengths and skills that support the business goals. As Jean grew more frustrated with Diana's attitude and emotional demands, she told Trixie that she wanted Diana out of the business. Trixie knew how hurt Diana would be, but she also realized Diana was not pulling her weight. Trixie agreed to write a letter, with Jean, in which they would tell Diana she hadn't contributed an equal share and ask her to sell back her interest in the business.

Diana received the letter from the other two women and was devastated. She couldn't believe that friends could do this to her. She had thought that the friendship came first and that the business was a way to extend their personal connections. The goals and understandings of these three women regarding their business were different. Had they anticipated these differences and worked with them, they could have spared themselves pain and kept the friendship.

Diana felt rejected, not just as a business partner but as a person. For months she became a virtual recluse in the community, and when her husband had an opportunity to transfer to another city, she implored him to take the job so she could finally get away from the "self-interested" women who "don't know the meaning of friendship."

This painful experience left its mark on Trixie and Jean, now more partners than friends. Each came to understand that the old friendship no longer existed and that the needs of the business meant the women either produced or closed down. By the time of their first loan review, Jean offered to buy Trixie's interest in the business over a five-year period. "Never again will I try a business venture with friends," Jean says. "From now on I will work with employees—no confusion between business needs and friendship issues. It's cleaner that way, and far less painful when things don't work out."

I have met women who decided to end their business when that business became a threat to their friendship. When their consulting company faced a major growth issue, for example, Nina and Elizabeth had very different feelings about how to respond. The conflict affected their friendship and, rather than have fifteen years as friends end in a dispute over their business, they decided to sell to another consultant and return to their friendship base.

Too often, however, women who go into business together as friends discover too late that the professional and personal relationships prove challenging. Women need to learn to confront these issues during the planning stages of a business and to be absolutely open about their expectations for the business and for each other.

When Betty Brown, Gail Thomason, and I began our writing and training business in 1983, we developed a questionnaire for each other. We asked if we saw the business as a job or a career. We asked about expectations for making money, about needs and values. We talked about how we would relate to each other and agreed that, to maintain focus on the business, we would not socialize after hours unless the event had a business context. We discussed our children and how present they would be on the phone or in person during the work day. We defined our roles within the business and our expectations for performance. In essence, we talked through an agreement that made it comfortable for us to be friendly without confusing friendship expectations with our business goals. Gail has since moved to another city; but even after seven years, Betty and I continue to appreciate each other as business partners and enjoy a friendly working relationship.

After I described our relationship during a workshop presentation, a woman raised her hand to ask me a "personal" question. "Aren't you hurt," she asked, "when you know Betty is having a party or going out to lunch and you aren't invited?" "No," I answered her without hesitation. "I'm not hurt at all. I appreciate that Betty and I allow each other the freedom to pursue our own social and personal lives. We care about each other and we care about our business. Our professional relationship protects what we value and has allowed us to work compatibly and productively for over ten years!"

Creating Work Friends

Work friendships offer women a new type of relationship. We can learn to enjoy the company of women we work with while reserving our more intimate friendships for women outside our workplace. Within a work context we can share laughter, moments from our personal lives, gestures of caring, and occasions for recreation. We can offer each other understanding and support while reserving the deeper expressions of friendship for friends not connected with our jobs.

Jenna, an accounts manager, provides a positive example of how women can approach their work friendships. "I have always understood the difference between work-friends and true friendships," she told me at the end of a workshop. "Perhaps it is an intuitive thing with me. I want to protect myself, and I want to protect the women I meet and am attracted to for friendship. While I'm working with these women, I maintain a friendly but slightly formal relationship. We get to know one another and care about each other's feelings, but we go home to our own lives.

"What is interesting, though," Jenna went on to say, "is that some of my work-friends are now my closest, dearest friends." She explained that after she moved to another branch or company, she would "cycle back," as she put it, and get to know her old work-friends in a new, more intimate way. Having been friendly in the first place established a base from which the deeper friendship could later grow.

Respecting the limits of a work-friend relationship may mean moments of loneliness for people like Jacqueline, director at Educational Testing Services; however, as she says, "It's the only alternative if you want to avoid problems." As with Jenna, understanding the difference between a work-friend and a traditional friend seems to Jacqueline almost intuitive. "I'm happy working with women I like," says Jacqueline," but I'm aware of the fine line, especially when I'm the one in the supervisory position. When a group of us from work goes out for dinner, of course we end up talking about the men in our lives and other non-work topics. It feels good to connect this way. But these women have never been to my home, that would seem too close. Yes, sometimes over a weekend I feel lonely and would like a long talk with a good friend, but not with women from work. Maybe they will come to my house sometime, but only if I have a party for the whole office and invite these women as part of the group."

Louise McCoy, formerly with the Peace Corps and now owner of a gourmet food and specialty kitchen shop in California, echoes Jacqueline's caring and restraint. "I can do business with people not my friends, but I have a tendency to make friends with everyone I work with. These friendships are different, however, from the sit-in-a-mud-bath, laugh-at-our-foibles friendship I share with a group of women I have known since college. I understand the importance of professional distance, and that's how I keep work friendships friendly."

Balancing friendship needs and workplace demands in a work friendship may not be easy for all women. We must learn, though, how to reach this balance if we are to protect ourselves and women we care about from confusion and betrayals. Work friendships, like traditional friendships, are gifts we must honor, respect, and celebrate.

In order to maintain work friendships, it's also important to cultivate and nurture friendships outside of work. With our non-work friends we can share without hesitation who we are, what we feel, and what we need. We can extend our families to include these friends, and we can enjoy the nurturing that comes from those with whom we can be intimate and affectionate.

As busy as we are in today's world, pursuing friendships outside of work takes planning and commitment. For those of us who have lived in a community before starting to work, we may have strong friendships already in place. For those of us new to an area, we may want to join clubs or church groups or become involved in volunteer work to meet women who will share our interests and become our friends. For all of us, we need to plan to keep our friendships current and alive.

My friend Dede and I have bought a series of tickets for plays together. Before each play, we meet for dinner and indulge in a good talk before crossing the street to the theater and taking our seats. Without this commitment to get together, I am sure our busy schedules would keep putting obstacles in our paths and we would miss the warmth and support our friendship gives us.

Suggestions for Work Friendships

My partners, Betty and Barbara, and I have work friendships. We like and respect each other while honoring

prescribed limits that protect us from becoming too personally involved with, or emotionally dependent on, each other.
The following guidelines have helped us maintain the boundaries between work friendships and traditional friendships.
They also reflect what we have learned from other women
who have successfully managed this sensitive balance:

* Enter the workplace expecting to be friendly, but not
demanding friendship. Remember that friendship involves
risk and that, for many women, work priorities must come
first over friendship considerations.

* Keep activities with work-friends work-related. It's
fun to go out after work to relax, laugh, and exchange stories
about our families or other people in our lives. This gives us
an opportunity to build up a reserve of positive feelings to
carry us over rough spots when later we find ourselves in the
throws of a bad day. Bowling or volleyball teams made up of
friends from work allow us to get together for fun while
keeping work in mind. It's when we begin sharing family
gatherings or non-work-related social time with work-friends
that we create opportunities for expressing ourselves in ways
we may later regret. It is difficult for us, after flirting at a party
or yelling in frustration at a resistive child, to re-establish our
workplace image and demeanor come Monday morning.

* When approaching friendship at work, be willing to
talk with other women about conflicts and challenges such a
relationship can entail. Be open in anticipating competition
issues, time demands, favoritism, and potentials for betrayal.
Open communication early in a friendship can help positive
relationships survive.

* Care, but limit what you share. We can be caring
toward our work friends, but we need to be conscious of what
we share in the way of intimacies and emotional expectations. Sharing stories of our vulnerabilities and weaknesses,
as friends do when seeking consolation and understanding,

may create an image of ourselves that could compromise our effectiveness at work. For example, with your work-friend you might want to explain why you are tired or irritable. You could comfortably tell her that you and Scott have been confronting some problems and that it has taken a toll on your energy. However, you might want to think twice before sharing with her that you feel totally raw and exhausted because Scott has been seeing Krista again—you don't know why you stay with him, but you're scared to be alone and you can't gain control of yourself. Sharing this much threatens your image as a woman in charge of yourself, and that could make your friend uncomfortable switching from an intimate to a professional relationship during working hours.

8

Taking It
Personally

"If there is one thing that makes working with women difficult, it's that they take everything so personally! They're so sensitive, you have to double-think every word. We'd get so much more accomplished if women could be less emotional and more rational!"

A man didn't say this. A woman did—and she is not alone in feeling this way. Almost one-third of the women answering our survey identified emotional sensitivity, or "taking it personally," as a problem for women working with women. "Women read too much into everything," one woman wrote. Others commented: "Women give personal meaning to every work situation. They get their feelings hurt too easily. They're too touchy. They spend more time reacting than working. They hold grudges. They're too emotional. They can't stay rational!"

Women's sensitivity is our strength. We make an effort to establish personal relationships with our colleagues. We

187

care about the feelings of others. We encourage growth of our co-workers and invite them to participate in information sharing and decision making. We can read a situation quickly and know who's within and who's outside the team. We recognize the whole person, not just the job or function she performs. As we and others have noted, this gives us tremendous advantages at work.

Our sensitivity to others and to situations, however, can also create problems for us when we let our emotional reactions dominate our rational responses. Before going on, please take a minute to read the following questions and answer "yes" or "no."

_____ When people criticize your work, do you feel as if they are criticizing you?

_____ If you are transferred to another work group, do you immediately imagine you have done something wrong?

_____ If your boss doesn't like your idea, do you conclude she doesn't like you?

_____ If your manager reprimands you for having brought the wrong statistics to a meeting, do you assume she doesn't like you?

_____ When your suggestions are vetoed, are your feelings hurt?

_____ If you lose a promotion, do you feel your self-worth is shattered?

_____ If your proposal has been rejected, do you feel you are a failure?

_____ When someone suggests you take a course to refresh or add a skill, do you feel offended?

_____ If you do not receive the vacation schedule you requested, do you feel taken advantage of?

_____ If you are not consulted on an issue, do you feel hurt and left out?

If you answered "yes" to any of these questions, you know what it's like to overpersonalize at work. (If you don't answer "yes," please consider that these situations do describe some, perhaps many, of the women you interact with at work.) Overpersonalizing means taking personally comments or criticisms that others might see as emotionally neutral. When we overpersonalize, we do not separate who we are from what do or produce. We process criticism as personal attacks, and we blame ourselves irrationally for circumstances beyond our control or responsibility.

Overpersonalizing isn't something we choose, either for ourselves or for the women with whom we work. But it happens, and when our emotions do take over, we "do gender" and therefore are more likely to act out those feelings with women than with men. That's because, with men, we've learned how to keep our personalizing to ourselves. However, when we interact with women, we expect what's historically been acceptable within a female context. For good or for ill, we feel more comfortable being ourselves with women and so don't hide or suppress our feelings.

That's why, although criticism from a male co-worker can hurt our esteem, and we may bristle and withdraw to recoup our composure—we are unlikely to strike back and make him pay. We accept the criticism and then go on. With women, however, we expect, or at least we would like to believe, that they will always make us feel appreciated. When they don't, we respond by punishing them for having hurt us. And when one woman responding at an emotional level tangles with another woman reacting emotionally, productive work may stop until the fur settles and comfort is reestablished.

Recent research on brain organization may help explain why women have trouble separating the emotional from the rational. In *Brain Sex: The Real Difference Between Men and Women*, Anne Moir and David Jessel review research by Sandra Whitleson relating to characteristics of male and female brains. According to Whitleson, in a male brain, emotional capacity is centered in the right hemisphere only. In the female brain, the ability to recognize emotional content in a situation exists in both the right and the left hemispheres. Whitleson's findings suggest that men can better keep emotions separate from reason and have more control keeping emotional and rational responses distinct.

Women, in contrast, can't easily ignore the information we're receiving about the emotional context of a situation. We have no "emotion-free" zone. Our brain's ability to read the emotional element in a voice, or a gesture, gives us an advantage over men in that we can detect and interpret the emotional nuances in personal and work-related interactions. Some researchers even propose that this capacity may help explain "women's intuition."

But with this advantage comes a challenge. There are certain situations when we would prefer to control, or eliminate, the emotional responses that distract us from an appropriate focus and make productive workplace function difficult for us and our coworkers.

Managing Our Sensitivity

As women, we can learn to control our emotions without losing the sensitivity that supports our relationships with people. The first step is an internal process: we need to be aware when we personalize workplace interactions. The second step is an external one: we need to control how we express our emotions when we interact with people at work.

Learning to "Spectate"

One of Barbara's goals in working with women is to help them learn to depersonalize their responses by separating their emotional reactions from the rational context. Often what sends a woman to see Barbara on a work-related issue is a remark or situation the client took personally. "My job," Barbara explains, "is to help the client step back and look at the situation rationally. I call it spectating on emotions."

To spectate on your emotions, Barbara suggests the following approach: If you conclude that your boss doesn't like you because she says on Friday she needed the reports last Tuesday and you still haven't finished, step back and spectate on how you're reacting. Accept that for the moment you feel hurt because she criticized you. Accept that you may have failed her expectations. Then ask yourself to look at the situation rationally. Is being liked and getting your work done on time and *really* connected? Or was your boss simply stating a fact about when she needed the reports and asking you to have them on time in the future?

Getting work done on time and being liked do not have to be connected. Being asked to turn in reports on time is a reasonable, necessary request. A healthy response would be for you to assess why your work was late and to change the way you handle your work load in the future. You'll be pleased to discover your new level of productivity and your boss will have no reason to criticize. You can choose to be rational. You don't have to succumb to an emotional response.

Not only do some women overpersonalize criticisms and commands, but sometimes we take personally situations that aren't even directed at us as individuals! Again, Barbara suggests that learning to spectate on our emotional responses can help us achieve a more rational perspective and approach. She uses Lynn's story to illustrate the point.

Lynn felt her company was out to get her personally. Her anger focused on a "comp-time" rule that wouldn't allow her to take time off on Mondays that were her children's school holidays. Her emotional response to this restriction made her hate her company because she felt it didn't care about her. Yet, she couldn't afford to walk away from the salary and the benefits.

Barbara helped Lynn to recognize how her feelings of anger kept her from seeing the whole picture: that the system was impersonal, it wasn't trying to be mean to her as an individual, and that the rules of the company had existed since before she began to work there. By spectating on her emotions, Lynn was able to depersonalize her response and accept the restrictions. And in taking a reasonable approach, Lynn was eventually able to work out a "comp-time" arrangement that worked for her and her children. "It's difficult for some women to withdraw their emotions," Barbara concludes. "Yet, when they succeed, they improve their comfort level and their ability to function and produce."

So next time you feel your emotions rising at work, you can choose to back away and spectate on your reactions. You can explain the situation to yourself rationally, and you can then choose a response that corrects the problem and eliminates future misunderstandings.

Distancing

Spectating allows us to look at the rational as well as the emotional issues to gives us some perspective. Distancing lets us separate ourselves emotionally from our products or our ideas so we don't overpersonalize when our work is criticized or our suggestions rejected.

Distancing means putting a space between what you

produce and who you are. When you distance yourself from your work, you say to yourself: My promotion plan is not me. I can put my plan over there, and I am still here. I can walk away from my plan and am still whole. I can look at that plan objectively. I can even bring forward the plan to a group as if I am presenting someone else's work. I can respond to suggestions for making the plan better and learn how to work more effectively myself in the future.

Savannah, a marketing project manager, admits she has made herself miserable in the past by personally identifying with criticism of her work. The last time it happened during a presentation, she came nearly to tears and experienced a "momentum paralysis."

"I was scheduled to present ideas for a product promotion plan to our new work group, made up entirely of females!" she tells. "I had not yet established a relationship with these women, and as they began to attack my ideas, my hands started to shake and my face tightened. I couldn't control my thoughts. I interpreted every question or criticism as an attack against me. My immediate manager was at the presentation and saw what was happening. She interrupted the meeting, saying that the input had been good and postponed further discussion until I had had time to revise the plan. I was embarrassed by my behavior. I shouldn't have let them get to me, for when I did, I became more vulnerable. I could have talked myself into a less emotional position. It was then that I became determined to detach myself from my work. Now, when I present a plan, I pretend I'm a consultant presenting someone else's idea. I pretend it's not my baby. If the baby or the method gets attacked, I'll listen and respond rationally. I stay detached—and I stay in control. Distancing works, and I'm a better team player for having learned it."

Distancing gives us a way to depersonalize a situation and function effectively in critical situations. It can also help those of us who hesitate to make suggestions or offer opinions for fear of being rejected as incompetent or "foolish." If you know you are not your ideas, you can contribute more easily.

When I asked Cecile, a master teacher, if overpersonalizing affected the teachers she worked with, she focused on lost input and ideas from women because they were too afraid to contribute. Women, she told me, often had great ideas for new programs or valuable insights on community issues influencing school policy. But, she claimed, she had too often watched men march forward to the principal and present their ideas while the women talked among themselves, gathering consensus but not action. The women, she concluded, couldn't separate themselves from their ideas and weren't willing to risk having their ideas—and themselves—criticized or rejected. Out of self-protection, they kept their ideas to themselves, or among themselves. The men who could better separate themselves from their ideas were heard and eventually recognized for their contribution.

Too many good ideas stay buried in women's conversations because we haven't known how to encourage each other to go forward and make our thoughts public. But we can learn.

Just as distancing ourselves from our projects can help us depersonalize a review session, so can distancing ourselves from our ideas help us depersonalize the criticism or rejection that might follow. What happens when someone says "no" to an idea? It's the idea, not us, they've rejected. We're still standing and very likely noticed and valued for having contributed toward defining or solving a problem. By controlling our irrational fear of rejection, we will get the recognition we deserve for good thinking. By depersonalizing our connection with our ideas, we will be more likely to contribute more of our input in whatever system, school or business we work.

For Peggy Reeves, representative to the Colorado State Legislature, detachment comes naturally. "If I took criticism and rejection personally," she says, "I wouldn't be able to accomplish my goals." If Peggy has a bill and it loses, instead of feeling wounded, she asks herself, "What arguments could I have worked harder on? Whose point of view did I need to consider so if I introduce the bill again, it will pass?" By posing questions to herself in this way, Peggy accomplishes a distance from the personal that allows her to get her job done. She thinks in terms of "the bill," not "me," and the distancing works.

One of our strengths as working women comes from our ability to connect with and care about our jobs and our products. We do become emotionally committed to our work, and this involvement encourages our performance. However, too much personalizing means we lose control of the focus we need to keep working effectively. Distancing can help us achieve and maintain a workable balance.

Self-Talk

Self-talk has also helped women we work with get beyond overpersonalizing. Similar to spectating on our emotions, self-talk takes a comment and translates it into emotionally neutral language.

So, for example, if your sales manager says, "Wanda, your presentation needs work. Your slides are too cluttered. No one could follow what you're offering when they can't keep up with your facts and figures," get rid of the "you." "You" makes us feel we've been attacked. Reword what she said, using self-talk to detach and emphasize the positive. Tell yourself, "She wants the presentation to improve and she's telling me how to do it better. She said people like uncluttered slides. She said they will follow the presentation better if the charts and graphs are simple and easy to read. She cares about my success. I'll work on my presentation."

Positive self-talk also helps when we catch ourselves making irrational, personalized assumptions about workplace situations that aren't going our way. For example, if you wanted a promotion and didn't get it, rather than telling yourself, "They simply don't like me. They overlook me. They don't think I fit in here, so they never give me a chance," step back and talk through the situation in a rational, positive manner. Say "I wanted to be selected for the management position, but I never told anyone directly. They required that to be selected, an employee had to have twelve hours of training during the year. I hadn't taken any classes. I'll sign up today for the level one course, then I'll try for the promotion when I've completed all twelve hours."

Self-talk and distancing help keep overpersonalizing under control. We serve ourselves well and make a positive contribution to women working together when we resist "taking it personally."

Balancing Politeness and Directness

We can learn to control our irrational responses at work. But what about the other women who act our their emotions with us as their target? What can we do to prevent another woman taking our remarks or actions personally? How can we help control the balance between sensitivity and rationality when we work with other women? One way is to continue using the indirect, polite communication style we learned as girls, but to balance that style with clear directions and product-focused criticisms.

Women's emotional sensitivity may offer a partial explanation for the polite, indirect communication style some researchers identify as typically female. In the current enthusiasm to define male and female communication styles, much has been made about male directness and female indirectness. Men, we are told, issue commands and criticisms directly, without the couching language intended to make others feel comfortable with the message. Women, researchers say, use a more polite approach with other people, requesting instead of demanding and tagging statements with "okay?" or "is that right?" to soften the impact of our assertiveness.

One linguistic argument is that our politeness results from our being in an inferior position within the male/female culture. "Men's language," Berkeley professor Robin Lakoff writes, "is the language of the powerful. It is meant to be direct, clear, succinct, as would be expected of those who need not fear giving offense."

Relative power positions certainly influence how we select language to get what we want and serve our needs. But there may be longer term objectives than just power that also influence our communication style. "Granted, women have lower status than men in our society," Deborah Tannen writes in *You Just Don't Understand: Men and Women in Conversation*. "But this is not necessarily why they prefer not to make outright demands. The explanation for a woman's indirectness could just as well be her seeking connection." By being direct, not being polite, we risk offending others and losing relationships, for an hour or a day, or for the duration of our time working together. As Professor Emeritus Jessie Bernard explains in *Toastmaster*, "Traditionally, the cultural norms of femininity and womanliness have prescribed appreciatively expressive talk or stroking for women . . . they were to raise the status of the other, relieve tension, agree, concur, comply, understand, accept."

The good news tells us that in the workplace at least, women are able to "code switch," communicating sometimes in the female style and in other circumstances borrowing from the male style. We use our polite style to solicit involvement, motivate co-workers, and maintain positive relationships. We can also, when working with both men and women, switch to the male style and use direct, assertive language to communicate what we want people to do and to tell them what we are thinking. Code switching serves us well; however, women who choose a direct style with other women can leave their subordinates and co-workers feeling attacked and uncomfortable. Their direct style can work against the positive relationships they hope to accomplish.

I was having lunch with a group of women from Edna's accounting department when a reference to Edna's direct style produced a unanimous response. Though the women said they appreciated Edna's openness and honesty, they felt uncomfortable when she gave them instructions or criticized their performance. If she had a problem with a deadline or quality of a presentation, she went directly to the responsible individual and said what she had on her mind. Becky spoke for the others when she said, "I like knowing she comes directly to me and that she doesn't go behind my back and complain to others on the project, but I wish she didn't make me feel so attacked, so inadequate. I can't feel comfortable with her when she doesn't seem to care about my feelings. I try not to be sensitive but I am. Sometimes it takes me all day to recover from one of her assaults!"

Though Edna doesn't mean to hurt Becky or the others, her directness often produces hurt feelings. Psychologist Mary Kay Biaggio notes that, "When under verbal attack, men tend to become angry while women tend to feel hurt." Anger expresses itself openly. Hurt festers and can subtly distract a woman from her best performance until, as Barbara explains, "something happens, a compliment or a kind word, to restore her esteem and positive feelings about herself."

When we choose to use a direct style with another woman, we need to consider how she might personalize our confrontation and react emotionally. To help her manage the moment and to preserve good working relationships for everyone, we can carefully select the words we use to deliver our message. We can also take the time to assure we have communicated our point effectively and to leave the other person with a positive sense of her worth and an understanding of what she needs to do to meet our expectations.

Dealing with Sensitive Co-Workers or Employees

In an ideal world, we and the women we work with would always be able to retain our sensitivity while controlling our tendency to overreact emotionally to the most innocent of comments. However we don't live in an ideal world, so we need to be prepared to deal with the emotional reactions of other women when they occur.

Mirella shared an example with me that sounds all too familiar. She had recently joined a new team that was just beginning plans to develop a new product. Feeling frustrated with the slow beginning, she admits to "not being my most sensitive self." She reverted to her natural style, which she describes as "direct, to the point, definitely not sweet and gentle," and confronted her team members, demanding to know who was responsible for developing the timeline.

That afternoon, Bev, who had prepared the timeline charts, brought them to Mirella's office. The charts, Bev explained in a brittle voice, had been distributed early in the week. "If you had checked your mail," Bev snapped at Mirella, "you would have found them." Mirella thanked Bev for the information and apologized for having missed the memo. Bev left the office without comment and avoided any contact with Mirella for the rest of the day.

The next morning Mirella tried to talk with Bev and explain why she had approached the chart issue the way she did. She apologized again for her abruptness, and she complimented Bev on her thoroughness. To no avail. Bev continued her silent treatment, and tension in the department rose to crackling. "That night," Mirella confessed embarrassedly, "I found myself at 10 o'clock baking a batch of cookies so I could leave them on her desk the next day."

By the time Mirella and Bev were working comfortably together again, with help from another team member, they had "essentially lost three valuable days soothing feelings and getting everyone comfortable again." Bringing focus back to the job and their need to rely on each other's knowledge got Mirella and Bev back on track. Mirella's willingness to apologize and Bev's eventual willingness to accept the apology also helped in working through the emotional reactions. But taking it personally cost the project time, and at work, time is money.

Sue Phillips, an experienced manager, is concerned about the time she spends working to fix relationships between women. "Women," she says, "spend a lot of time replaying what happened during exchanges with other people. They feel everything personally and come to me because they need to share what happened. I take the time to listen and to help them get to feeling okay about themselves again. Sometimes I think I spend as much time bolstering esteem as I do managing a department."

Louise, a small business owner, builds on the same theme. "When David, one of my employees, muffs up," Louise reports, "Dorlise, another employee, complains to me that I have not reprimanded him properly. I ignore her because I feel the matter is over and, besides, I am the boss. Then Dorlise feels criticized or rejected and begins asking me if everything is all right between us. As nicely as I can, and through gritted teeth, I respond, 'Yes, except that you're taking too much time, always asking me if everything's all right.'"

We cannot always prevent women we work with from overpersonalizing. We need to understand when an emotional reaction is someone else's problem and not our fault or responsibility. If we let ourselves be drawn into to a Bev's or a Dorlise's catastrophe every time their feelings get hurt, we lose valuable time and patience! What we can do, however, is to anticipate situations that have potential for causing an emotional response and deliver our messages in the most effective ways possible.

Just as self-talk can focus comments and criticism away from ourselves and direct them more appropriately to our work or ideas, so too can the language we use with other women help them view their situations more objectively. One way is to get rid of the accusing "you" when we talk. Instead of saying to Helene, "You can't seem to get through to the patients," try "Helene, patients appreciate hearing clear reasons why they should follow our instructions." Then emphasize what actions she can take to improve her output or increase her skill base. That way she'll be more willing to take your suggestions because you aren't attacking her.

Performance reviews, according to a number of women supervisors and managers I interviewed, can be especially difficult with sensitive women. Women from their twenties to their sixties tell me they spend almost twice as long in performance evaluation sessions with women than men! Part of the time is taken up being polite, using carefully selected language to deflect attention from a personal attack and protect self-esteem. The rest of the time is spent listening to emotional reactions and moving attention from criticism to what-happens-next. For everyone, action is the best antidote to criticism. Men tend to be more action-oriented, taking an "all right, now what do I do" approach. Women may need more help moving from a personalized, emotional response to "what do I do about it?"

Successful women managers tell me that they prepare before a performance review that contains criticism or suggestions for improvement. They practice focusing on the work or the issue (being a team player, for example) and have a plan of action in mind to help the employee improve. This way, the person receiving the review leaves the session with a plan to follow, a way to take charge and reestablish confidence and esteem. Planning what you will say and what you will suggest as a follow-up can help control an overpersonalized response. When we don't have to take time away from our work to assuage the feelings of overly-sensitive women, everyone comes out ahead.

PMS

"Great," a friend interjected when I reviewed this chapter with her. "You give us some good ideas about managing our own overpersonalizing and helping other women control their responses, but what about those days when, try as we will, we just can't control our emotions? What about PMS?"

In the last ten years enough research has hit the media to convince even the most resolute skeptics that women's hormonal cycles do affect our moods. For those of us mildly afflicted, that may mean mild depression, vulnerability to tears, or heightened irritability. For others with more severe symptoms, tempers flare, depression overwhelms, and trivial remarks spark violent reactions.

If you suffer from PMS, the best you can do under these circumstances is to keep track of the calendar and anticipate the mood swings. When the tears well or irritability spikes, remind yourself why and take time to count backwards from ten to one. You may save your composure and protect some unsuspecting co-worker from a barrage of criticisms or a litany of doomsday predictions.

It may help to tell your female co-workers that it's PMS time—to give yourself, and them, a distance zone. And you can return the consideration by noting that when chocolate M&Ms appear on Sheila's desk, you should back off from applying unnecessary pressure.

However, keep in mind the difference between explanations and excuses. You can explain emotional outbursts, but that doesn't guarantee others will accept the excuse. Women completing our survey weren't universally sympathetic to the hormonal defense. One woman wrote she was "sick of the PMS excuse." Another jotted "PMS—someone always has it, or believes she does." One woman we surveyed had no trouble identifying three negative factors about working with women. She simply wrote, "Hormones, hormones, hormones. When will women learn to keep them to themselves?"

Reality Partners

In working with women prone to overpersonalizing, we can take time to resolve conflicts and smooth ruffled esteem. We can control our language to focus on situations and not people. We can tread cautiously when the chocolate flags go up. And, most effectively, we can agree to help one another keep both the emotional and the rational in perspective.

When we have done all this, there is still one more positive thing we can do—we can find a "reality partner" who will talk with us about these issues and help us gain perspective. Sari uses a such a partner. She and another woman have agreed to provide each other with reality checks when they feel their emotions or the tendency to overpersonalize are stalling them. "I'll go to Joan," Sari explains, "and ask her if I'm reading too much into the abrupt way Glen or Charlotte dismissed my suggestion for getting another bid. Then Joan can remind me that Charlotte has a deadline and has been working twelve-hour days. I'll then stop worrying that she has a specific case against me.

"I do the same for Joan. When she didn't get the project assignment she wanted and felt like a total failure, as if no one thought she had any value, I helped her focus objectively. We looked at her background and at the experience they needed for the team. It made rational sense to choose someone who had worked with foreign markets, and Joan hadn't done that. Her goal now is to work toward an opportunity to get that experience."

My partner Betty adds here that one advantage for women in developing a network of associates within and outside work is that we gain the resources of many "reality partners." Once when working with a difficult woman, Betty decided that before taking Shara's attitude personally, she would seek a second opinion. She called another consultant, Elena, who had worked with Shara and asked her how she responded to Shara's style. "You're not out in left field," Elena reassured her. "Shara's just not in the real world when it comes to training costs and billing procedures." Using Elena as a reality partner helped Betty approach Shara objectively and resolve the cost issue successfully.

As Betty's experience demonstrates, we don't have to rely only on one "reality partner." As women work with women, we can encourage our co-workers to let us know when emotions or overpersonalizing are getting in the way of performance. Sari's manager did that when she interrupted the personal attacks by the other women during Sari's presentation of the product promotion plan. Inga, her manager, saw that emotions were getting out of hand and called a halt before the feelings escalated out of control. Sari appreciated her check and so did the other women.

Eugenia Ortega, a Ph.D. candidate and California Youth Authority treatment team supervisor, told us how she would want to see women confront each other when emotions flare or personalizing impairs productive work. "On occasion I have found myself enmeshed in such circumstances. The best approach would probably be to have other women call our attention to what's happening. This would, in turn, require that the women involved in the emotional issue be willing to receive comments and criticism from their co-workers. This could be tough for women already operating at an emotional level. More criticism isn't what they need; but if it's done sensitively and with the purpose of helping everyone get back to task, it can work. Regaining control and the satisfaction of accomplishing good work are worthy rewards."

Suggestions to Avoid Overpersonalizing

* If you find yourself reacting emotionally to a situation . at work, use the techniques suggested in this chapter: learn to spectate on your emotions; try to distance your personal self from the work you perform; find a reality partner to help you gain perspective on your emotional responses. You may also want to make a personal inventory of words, phrases, and behaviors that trigger an emotional reaction in you. The next time you find yourself beginning to react to these cues, stop, count to ten, and assess the situation from a rational perspective.

* If you work with someone who overreacts emotionally, know the limits of what you can do to guide her rational responses. Realize that her emotional reactions are hers and

not yours. Don't be drawn into lengthy, unproductive, exhausting emotional exchanges. Stay focused on the objective realities and the behaviors that will allow each of you to achieve your goals.

* Develop strategies for eliminating, or at least reducing, the potential for other women to overpersonalize your remarks. Avoid the accusing "you," and keep the situation, not the person, the object of your concern. This approach helps us separate what we do from who we are.

* If you believe you respond to situations too personally and want to take charge of your emotions, Barbara suggests you read *Where You End and I Begin*, by Anne Katherine, MA (Parkside Publishing Co., 1991).

9

Getting Along with One Another

Kay, a bright woman moving up through the management ranks of a large corporation, unexpectedly decided to take an early retirement option. I asked her why, when she had been so successful, she wanted to leave her job and her company. "They don't like me," she said, fighting back tears. "I get along with the men fine; they admire my ability. But the women, they just don't like me! I have tried being nice. I even lent one of the women my new suit for a presentation in Boston. I may be hard-driving, but that's my style. Why can't they just accept that and like me?"

Kay isn't alone in wanting to work in an environment where women like each other. Lenya also considered leaving her job, but not because other women didn't like her. Lenya wanted to leave because she didn't like one of the women on her work team. "That woman walks into the room and I can't concentrate on what I'm doing," she tells me. "Her tone of voice, those exaggerated gestures, the way she tells people what to do! I can't stand her. I'd quit if I could, and maybe

209

I will anyway. I can't work with a woman I don't like."

In the last chapter, I talked about how women at work can learn to use spectating, distancing, and self-talk to depersonalize the occasional remarks that make us feel inadequate or angry. As a result, we gain control and the work goes on. But what about working day after day with women whose style, attitude, and presence irritate us beyond tolerance and make our work hours miserable? Just as options exist for us to depersonalize the emotional impact of everyday workplace confrontations, so do possibilities exist for us to work productively with people who don't like us and whom we don't like.

This is a particularly difficult issue for women because women like to be liked—and we like to like other women. "In The Female System," Anne Wilson Schaef reminds us, "the center of the universe is relationship. Everything must go through, relate to, and be defined as relationship." And of course, what draws people together and keeps them in a relationship is that they like each other. When women who work together don't like each other, the ensuing discomfort makes working together stressful and threatens good performance.

Without connecting, without relationship, many women cannot experience sustaining satisfaction with their work or with their jobs. Research on job satisfaction for men and women repeatedly identifies human relations factors as being more important to women than to men. In an article for *Working Women*, Julia Kagen refers to a study in which 59 percent of the women sampled mentioned that one positive aspect of their jobs was working with people they like. Only 43 percent of the sampled men, however, identified working with people they liked as important to job satisfaction.

Women want to feel connected and appreciated at work. Responses to our survey tell us that women appreciate the personal factors of "understanding," "pleasantness," "similarity," and "support" that let us get along with and like each other. In contrast, men care most about achieving status within a group. And achieving that status depends more on proving his ability and commanding attention than on being liked and liking others.

The authors of *Brain Sex: The Real Difference Between Men and Women*, offer this observation: "Men come to the world of work with an acceptance of a world of arbitrary rules, and an experience of working collectively with people they may not like, but who are useful to them." They don't have to like someone in order to appreciate that she or he is getting the job done. On the other hand, Moir and Jessel continue, "Women who, as girls, chose their friends with much greater, and more committed, care, try to like the people they work with, understanding their needs, breaking down the barriers of status."

Barbara relates women's ability and need to see the whole person to the traditional female role as the nurturer. "Women," she tells us, "see skills and function as just one part of a person who also has feelings, needs, and potentials. To nurture the whole person, we must recognize the whole person. To focus only on what that child, or individual, can do or how she can function affects the meaning of relationship. We can't have personal, caring relationships with performing objects. And without relationships with whole people, many women feel incomplete and denied expression of their full personhood."

Though many women resist treating people as functioning units, adopting the male attitude of separating style from function may help us get beyond worries at work about being liked and liking others. First, though, we need to understand the difference between style and function. Style refers to the way we express ourselves, for example in social interactions, in dress, and in work habits. It has more to do with one's personality than with one's ability to read spreadsheets or manage a health benefits program. Of course, style may be a factor in one's ability to function successfully, in sales for example, but functions are not limited to particular styles. Successful managers, supervisors, health care professionals and teachers represent every style in the galaxy!

Men tend to see a person's function as the end in sight; women identify function as a step toward connection, not an end in itself. However, appreciating another woman's skills and strengths as separate from her style gives us a new way to build a whole-person relationship. We can base the relationship on respect for how she does her job, and we may eventually add personal feeling to what we value. We can even grow to like the woman who initially drove us to migraines.

When Other Women Don't Like Us

Most women are not in a position, as Kay was, to leave our jobs if we feel the women we work with don't like us. We need the salary: We don't want to give up our seniority or the chance to gain experience. Often, we simply enjoy our work and don't want to move elsewhere. However, work isn't like a school or the community. We can't just choose to ignore or avoid people we believe dislike us. Instead, we must manage the situation so that everyone can work more comfortably together.

When we sense that others at work may not like us, we do have choices of behavior other than quitting or making ourselves invisible. First, we must begin by accepting that not everyone will like us. Some people are drivers and others are followers, and not everyone will automatically get along. Second, we must learn to be fair to ourselves. We know when we're performing well and meeting our responsibilities to our teams and companies. Because someone doesn't like us does not mean we have failed across the board. It means, instead, that we have issues other than performance to consider if we want to increase our job satisfaction and improve our working relationships with others. Finally, we must accept that styles different from our own have their validity, and that, in fact, a workplace of people with diverse styles and approaches may be the most productive workplace of all!

Of course we would all rather be liked than disliked, but we can learn to accept that our job performance is more important than workplace popularity. We can also realize that others might eventually appreciate what we do even if at first they don't naturally like us. To help ourselves through the difficult moments when we feel hurt or angry, we can learn to depersonalize our responses to women who appear to dislike us. We must remind ourselves that not everyone will like our style; and that if we can look beyond style, others may follow our example. And we must also remind ourselves that some people who admire our performance also *do* like our style!

One way we can be leaders in looking beyond style and appreciating function is to not take offense when others telegraph their irritations with us or otherwise make us uncomfortable in a workplace context. To not take offense, says psychiatrist and author Christian Hageseth III, involves an "elegant way of counting to ten. When you experience an intense feeling, you discipline yourself to not respond with behavior. Instead you withdraw and reflect on the feeling. You 'take a walk' with the feeling and then thoughtfully consider appropriate behavior for response."

Hageseth adds that this reflective approach often leads to a discovery, about ourselves or about others, that can be very helpful in improving our relationships. In a very practical sense, not taking offense stops negative communication. We control our emotionally-based behaviors, and we help clear the air so everyone's attention can focus on the work at hand and the strengths each individual contributes.

I can't leave this section without a word of caution for women who believe the best way to deal with being disliked is to confront the issue directly. This might not be the best way to proceed. Let's see what might happen.

A woman like Kay who feels she is disliked might begin a confrontation by saying, "Emma, I feel you don't like me, and I think we should talk about it." This puts Emma in an awkward position. Perhaps she believes she had held her feelings in check and is both surprised and disturbed Kay picked up on the vibrations. Quite likely she will feel defensive, and if, in fact, she does dislike Kay, she may feel very uncomfortable discussing her reasons. If she hadn't given much thought to liking or disliking Kay, she may feel angry at Kay's assumption!

Women who have taken this direct approach to resolving their discomfort report that the confrontations often become emotional and resolve little. The women involved are left feeling exposed and self-conscious.

Confronting each other in this way usually works against creating an emotionally depersonalized environment, one in which mutual appreciation can lead to positive personal relationships. Emotionally charged confrontation is bad communication. Open, honest communication respects the situation and the individuals involved. Its purpose is to address issues and resolve conflicts, not to threaten others and make them defensive.

Women who still want to acknowledge discomfort within a relationship do, however, have an option. We can focus on specific behaviors when confronting a co-worker.

Instead of "You don't like me," we can begin with "Is there something I do, something in my style, that makes you uncomfortable?" With that kind of an opening, we may receive helpful feedback about our behaviors that we can then choose to apply to create a positive working environment for all our colleagues and co-workers.

Working with a Woman You Don't Like

Separating a woman's style from her job performance has proven an effective way for women to work with, and even grow to like, co-workers who initially drove them to Maalox! "Women may not always like other women because of their individual styles, enthusiasms, preferences, forms of humor, and the like," writes Jean Baker Miller, MD, in her classic, *Toward a New Psychology of Women*. "Of course, each woman does not have to like and enjoy all other women. Many women are developing a new spirit of appreciation of themselves and other women, recognizing the need for women to have a variety of ways of being themselves and being with others."

It was Miller's "spirit of appreciation" that helped my partner Betty and me come through some difficult days early in our partnership. I never disliked Betty; however, when we first began working together, we had to confront some style conflicts that almost defeated us.

From the moment I met Betty, I admired her self-assurance, her sense of humor, and her assertiveness. She is a down-to-business person who spends little time with non-productive frivolities. Her high energy level rides on a positive, optimistic attitude that believes all challenges represent opportunities. In contrast, I appreciate positive feedback to know that I am performing well. I enjoy casual chit-chat as a way of learning to care about people, and I apply a circumspect approach to new challenges.

Understandably, Betty became frustrated with my reluctance to approach people and openly market our business
at every civic or social event we attended. She knows the
importance of networking and enjoys the challenge of going
out and attracting new business. While I appreciate the value
of marketing as well, I prefer creating concepts and developing new materials that solicit clients and business.

When Betty left me "to-do" lists with names of people
to call or gave me suggestions for how to approach a new
client, I interpreted her instructions as criticism. I assumed
she considered me inadequate, and I resisted her efforts to
"control" me. She gave suggestions; I heard orders and
resisted complying. We both grew irritable; suddenly, our
communication, so vital to a partnership, became guarded,
abrupt, and protectively polite. Style conflicts were over-
whelming our necessary function, and coming to the office
meant experiencing more stress than satisfaction for both of
us.

Then we joined, at Betty's suggestion, a small business
development group. The facilitator of our group recom-
mended that we each take the Myers Briggs Type Indicator
test to discover our type, or style. We did. The test, designed
by Isabel Myers and her mother, Katherine Briggs, identifies
sixteen patterns, or types of personality, based on four pairs
of characteristics. Respondents' answers to questions show
how a person prefers to take in information, make decisions,
deal with the outside world, and seek an energy source. It
turned out that Betty and I represent personalities about as
different as a full dress parade and a solo stroll through the
forest. Not surprisingly, her preferences describe a field
marshal, whereas mine describe a person who is "intro-
verted," sensitive to contradictions, and potentially "obsessed with analysis."

Taking the Myers Briggs test forced us to look at our

styles in an objective, constructive way. The inventory depersonalized our conflicts and led us back to our function: growing a business together. We learned that our differences actually complemented each other. With this new understanding, I could now appreciate Betty's focus on the bottom line, her to-do lists, and the energy she communicates when addressing a workshop. In turn, she respects my preference for building client rapport one-on-one and my circumspect approach to analyzing business opportunities.

While at one point personalizing our style conflicts could have destroyed our business, separating style from function has allowed Betty's and my business to grow. While I once felt uncomfortable with the person who made me feel criticized and inadequate, I now like and appreciate the person whose qualities I admire.

What If She Drives You Crazy?

Betty and I had a relatively minor clash. But one day into your office, laboratory, hospital, or clinic may stride a woman whose style will signal intense friction. You won't be able to stand the way she slaps down her briefcase. She'll toss her hair in a flippantly confident manner that curls your fingernails. Her slow, monotone voice will blur your vision and fracture your attention. Your instant response says, "I can't work with this woman. I can't stand her. I hope she gets her expensive blazer caught in the elevator and the electricity blows." But no such luck. She's been hired, and she'll stay.

You may not have time for the Myers Briggs test or a seminar on difficult people. You will need help immediately before you crack a tooth or bolt for the door. Take a breath, step back, and study her style. A willingness to depersonalize, to separate her irritating behaviors from her skills and abilities, will help you to manage the situation and to work productively with a woman who might otherwise drive you crazy.

Try an exercise that has helped many women in our workshops. Write a list of the traits that bother you about her. Then, go back over the list and cross out any mannerisms or habits that have no effect on her ability to do her job—or interact with you on your job. For example, if she produces substandard work or withholds essential information from her co-workers, you have specific problems and have to confront her to accomplish change. But if she hums in the elevator or taps her pencil eraser when she makes a point, she can still function well as a supervisor, accountant, or design engineer.

The next step in this exercise is for you to analyze her strengths. List what she does well, even if you don't like the way she does it. Imagine why she was hired in the first place. Consider her skills, her experience. Observe where she succeeds with her work and with other people. Separate how she functions from your response to her.

Finally, ask yourself what this woman needs to function, what her comfort zones may be. Identify what's in it for you to work well with her: success on a mutual project, for example, or positioning yourself for advancement in the future. Identify what's in it for her to work well with you: she can get the information and feedback she needs, the department will run smoothly, etc.

Think "job," "work," "profession," "project"—not person. Keep your focus on the positive. Accept that your relationship with her is a workplace relationship, and that respecting her abilities might precede genuine feelings of care and concern. Respect forms the basis of many productive work-friendships. She whom we respect, we may eventually grow to like.

Lyda, a committed teacher, used this do-it-yourself

approach to get beyond a style conflict with her new principal, Maureen. Maureen had replaced a popular and respected woman who had served as mentor and friend to women and men on her staff. Entering this scene wasn't easy for Maureen, but her personality, so different from her predecessor's, set her up for style scrutiny—and resistance.

From Maureen's first all-too-chipper "good morning," Lyda knew she would not like this woman. The overly friendly facade didn't mesh with what quickly revealed itself as a controlling, domineering style. The new principal wanted to know what was happening in every classroom, in every program. Where the former principal had managed by being available for advice and assuming everyone was handling her or his teaching with a high degree of professionalism, this new principal wanted documentation of everything from schedules to parent contacts. Lyda felt challenged, demeaned, and intruded upon.

But it was the chilling voice that tightened Lyda's stomach and drove her into the supply closet to avoid being spotted when Maureen passed down the hall. Lyda carried home her resistance and dislike of the new principal. The thought of this woman observing her classroom distracted, almost obsessed, her. She spent more time plotting defiance than developing lessons. The image of Maureen haunted her even on her many jogs along the river.

Lyda considered leaving her job. Then she realized that to quit was not a solution. She loved her job, and did not want to sour or compromise all that was positive because she disliked one woman. Luckily, while jogging one day, her thoughts took a more productive turn. She worked her options through and decided to meet this woman on her playing field. She would discount the chipper exterior, the grating good will, and concentrate on delivering what this woman wanted. She would document her innovations and keep records of all materials requested and used. Instead of fighting a critique, she invited Maureen into her classroom and received the most perceptive review of her career. In listening to this woman's analysis of goals, objectives, and methods, Lyda discovered she respected her new principal's values and business/education sense.

Lyda became determined to focus on what she respected in Maureen's professionalism, not on trying to like her. She didn't expect or want Maureen to include her in her growing circle of overly friendly intimates. She did, though, expect to be valued and respected for her work as a master teacher.

The approach succeeded. With the pressure to like and be liked removed, Lyda could again focus on what she did exceptionally well: teach. Maureen recognized her talents and treated her with polite, professional respect. In return, Lyda benefitted from Maureen's experience and professional support. The voice chirping a melodious good morning still sets Lyda's smile on edge, but she discounts the style and concentrates on the substance.

We can't like every woman we work with, and not every woman will like us. To work productively together, to realize satisfaction while doing a job, depends on our determination to separate style from ability and contribution. Rather than run from a woman we can't stand, we can stop and assess her strengths. We can respect her for her abilities, and eventually we may grow to admire those qualities we respect.

I'm reminded of what Roz Spencer, an ebullient arts director, says to women who are intimidated by her direct style. When Roz raises her voice and a staff person complains, "You shouldn't yell at me," Roz responds, "I may get excited and raise my voice. That is my style. This is not an act against you; it is an expression of me." Those who work with

Roz and accept her style work with a knowledgeable woman in non-profit contemporary art promotion. They work with a woman who knows how to raise money and bring art to her community. They may not like her at first, but when they confront her strengths, they discover a mentor.

Liking isn't everything; neither is being liked. You can work with a woman who drives you crazy, and survive to applaud her.

Clash of Commitment Levels

Women seem to get along best at work with women who are like us or whose style and priorities seem compatible with our own. We like to surround ourselves with women who reinforce who we are. Varying commitment levels can create serious challenges for some women working with women. We bond with women whose priorities in balancing a career with family and community reflect our own, and we resent or distrust women whose commitment priorities are different.

Commitment has really not been an issue for men. For them, work is work; personal lives belong in another sphere. Women tend to merge work with the personal. Our personal connections lend strength and depth to our workplace relationships. When differences divide us, however, we lose the advantage of our merged and mutual power.

Since women began coming back to work in droves in the '70s, we have been conscious of how the male workplace perceives our dedication as well as our performance. We have been sensitive to the image women present to men based on our commitments. We have fought to be taken seriously, and when other women do not appear to be as committed, our frustrations can cause strong workplace tensions.

Louise, a former dean at Sonoma State University, remembers the frustration she experienced trying to encourage Jenny, a young secretary, to take advantage of free classes and opportunities to advance within the university structure. Jenny is one of a group of women whom I have heard referred to as "stratified and satisfied." Her attitude toward work contrasted with Louise's expectations for herself and for other women. "This woman made it very clear to me," Louise says, "that she wanted to be a secretary and nothing else. She also let me know that my constant suggestions that she make more of herself made her uncomfortable working with me. It was hard for me to recognize and acknowledge. After all, I was the associate dean of women and I believed all women wanted to advance as far as they could. It was difficult for me to accept that some women had other priorities and didn't see their careers as I saw mine."

In *Women vs Women: The Uncivil Business War*, Tara Roth Madden comes down hard on how women react to others with different priorities. She identifies three main groups of women who divide "white collar offices" into "Hate Squadrons." First, she defines the Careerists who put business concerns above personal concerns. Next come the Balancers, who strive to achieve harmony at home and at work. The last group Madden calls the Homing Pigeons, because they work only for the money and focus their energy primarily on returning home. Within each group are myriad subcategories.

"Women," Madden tells us, "generally develop antagonisms on the basis of these categories. Careerists are constantly at odds with Homing Pigeons, and both have trouble with Balancers, who cannot decide where their loyalties lie." Though not every woman aligns herself with a group and not every office becomes a cauldron of antagonism, conflicting commitment priorities do leave women feeling uncomfortable with each other. They may not respond with open hostility, but their tension can affect smooth communication. Any factors that create divisions among women hurt us, especially when we want to show that women are a force united, appreciative of one another and the good work we produce.

Jean and Cara represent two different commitment levels, though each holds the same job in loan processing for a regional bank. Jean's career-first commitment clashes with Cara's divided dedication between work and home. The women disapprove of each other's priorities even though they recognize each other's competence. Jean avoids Cara, distancing herself from a woman who she believes weakens opportunities for other women who plan—and need—to advance. Jean sees Cara's obvious connection with home as perpetrating the image of women as fragmented workers, unpredictable and incapable of 100 percent dedication.

Cara finds Jean unfeminine, even anti-woman. She can't relate to a woman who shows no concern for home and family but will spend sixty hours a week taking management classes, working late hours, and pouring over annual reports. Cara demeans Jean's priorities and devalues her successes as won by "unnatural" means. Their public discomfort with each other has raised tensions among the other women in the loan division who aren't always sure whose team they should join. As for Jean and Cara, their tensions inhibit a spontaneous exchange of ideas that could improve loan procedures and make the bank more successful.

Today, women face a new era. Corporations are beginning to accept that women and men are not alike, though each is capable of excellent work and dedication. To retain the best women in the future, corporations are becoming more flexible in allowing women—and men—to adjust their commitment priorities to their family and personal circumstances. The recently passed National Family Leave bill demonstrates an important step forward in this regard.

Felice Schwartz has spent thirty years researching women's advancement in the workplace. In her book *Breaking with Tradition*, she admonishes corporations to become more flexible in accommodating talented women and in making different commitment priorities respectable. "In some people, for example, the intensity of family drive will override career drive," she writes. "Then—and perhaps this is most important of all—you have to make that choice respectable. At some point you must allow them to make a lesser commitment, and to accept more limited rewards because they choose a lesser commitment. Don't discount them—in the present or for the future—because they have 'failed' in their commitment when in truth they are committed to your enterprise and at the same time to some other aspect of their lives."

Women also must not discount other women who do not demonstrate complete career dedication at all times in their lives. All of us are crucial elements in making the flexible corporation work. We must depersonalize our feelings when another woman's choices are different from our own. We must make her feel welcomed and appreciated for the talents and skills she contributes. When we value her performance and don't judge her choices, she will learn to offer us the same appreciation and support.

If Jeri had believed she had the support of other women, she might have requested a part-time position. Jeri works for a male-dominated corporation that avowedly prefers women who put their careers first. Jeri's manager, Gail, is married, has no children, and definitely puts her career above all else. A wonderful mentor, Gail encouraged Jeri to apply for promotions and gave her opportunities to prove her abilities. The other women in Jeri's department are fiercely protective of their career status, and Jeri feared that Gail and the others would feel she had let them down by Jeri's wanting to stay home part-time with her young children.

When Jeri made her decision, she went to Gail. To Jeri's surprise, Gail approached the situation positively. She talked about Jeri's work and the value of her talents to the projects she supported. If Jeri believed this was the right decision at this point, Gail supported her because, as she said, "we don't want to lose you." The other women have taken their cues from Gail and let Jeri know they value the work she contributes. When Jeri is again ready for a full-time commitment, she will be welcomed back.

Commitment choices will never be easy for women. Schwartz reminds us that "Career-and-family conflict is central to women, emotional, threatening, and both guilt-and anxiety-provoking." Women can help ease the threat and the anxiety by supporting each other's commitment decisions, helping to usher in a new era where what we contribute means more than why.

How well we perform our jobs, and how well other women perform theirs, must always come first at work. But as we learn about and appreciate the context of other women's lives, we can enhance our working relationships with each other. If we don't feel threatened or criticized, we can talk about our priorities. We can help each other with decisions and offer our support in a flexible workplace. Whether we have our sights on the top floor or our eye on the clock for when we can go home, we can all work well together.

Coping with Children

When I asked a group of insurance industry women for whom I was scheduled to give a talk what they considered the most critical issue in women working together, they told me, emphatically, "children." Most women with children cannot completely detach from those children during the workday. Whether in photos or conversations, on the phone or in the flesh, children appear at work. Their presence can create composure-curdling conflicts, especially among woman.

As women, we share the reality of children, whether we choose to exercise our biological potential or not. Those of us with children tend, to varying degrees, to assume that other women will understand what motherhood demands. We may expect men to become more understanding as they too balance family and work demands; but most of us don't test their tolerance at work with "kid stories" or requests to watch Sammy while we run to the printer. We do, however, expect this of other women, and it seriously affects how we get along with each other.

For some women, children have no place at work. For others, the inclusion of children in the workplace breaks down the boundaries between work and home, and helps to integrate the two worlds. In *The Female Advantage*, Sally Helgesen introduces Nancy Badore of Ford Motor Company. Nancy, executive director of the Executive Development Center, takes calls from her child's caretaker during meetings and brings the baby into the office. She represents women who believe integrating children and work "sends the message that we (women) think the . . . whole person is valuable. . . . That means the person as he relates to his family, not just his work. Work and family are part of who you are!"

Not everyone, however, is as euphoric about blending someone's motherhood dimension into the work day. Women without children can be uncomfortable knowing how to react to the child, and to the mother. They may find the presence of children more a distraction than an addition. And not every mother wants to deal with her own or other women's children during the time she has committed herself to work.

My partner Betty, for example, prefers to keep her work life and her life as a mother distinct. She cares deeply for her husband and sons, but she does not choose to discuss them while working. She prefers to focus intensely on projects at work and to discuss family during breaks. She does respect men and women who bring family to the workplace, but she does not need to know family details before working with clients. These details or family concerns do not drive her business relationships. Common goals do.

Women answering our survey identified common problems associated with children's presence at work. A number of respondents resented the time other women spend talking about children during working hours. Others focused their complaints on women who put their child's needs before their work responsibilities, leaving early or canceling meetings to accommodate a child's doctor's appointment or school performance. One woman wrote, "I can't stand the mothers who expect everyone to think they're martyrs because they have to come to work." And yet another told us, "Why should I care about someone's kids who have nothing to do with my life? It wastes time to talk about Jenny or Johnny when we need to bring the records up to date."

Confronting the issue of children in the workplace requires extraordinary tact. Any criticism of how we manage our children, or manage ourselves with our children, strikes at the heart of a mother's vulnerability. When Felice Schwartz says that the career/family conflict for women is "emotional, threatening, and both guilt-and anxiety-provoking," she also identifies why the presence of children at work can be such a delicate issue.

Schwartz' observation explains why the group of insurance women I spoke with agreed that children were the most important women-with-women issue in their offices. They were irritated with other women's children, and angry at how other women responded to their own children, but they were hesitant to approach the issue and hurt anyone's feelings! They would complain among themselves about a woman who was not present, but they would not confront her directly about her children.

Recently, some women in our office building let a child-at-work situation get out of hand because everyone was reluctant to get involved in an emotional confrontation. Shauna, the seven-year-old daughter of Kayla, a young financial advisor, would come to her mother's office after school. Kayla made sure Shauna knew not to disturb the men on the corridor. But she assumed the other women would understand her problem with after-school care and accept Shauna's presence.

Kayla let Shauna wander at whim, avoiding only the offices that contained men. Shauna would appear at our door modeling her Halloween costume or asking to borrow scissors. Not wanting to appear cold and heartless, we tolerated, just barely, the intrusions and told Shauna, ever so gently, to go play elsewhere because we were busy. However, having to interrupt a project to tell Shauna "not now" became increasingly irritating. We all avoided directly confronting Kayla.

Finally our secretary, who took the brunt of Shauna's attentions, asked the girl to return some marking pens and to stay in her mother's office. Kayla flared in Shauna's defense and instructed her daughter "not to talk to those women." We were all appreciative and relieved that our secretary had called the game, but we exchanged one tension for another. Kayla kept Shauna in her office after school but wouldn't speak to any of us on the floor. Before her lease was up, Kayla left the building, never saying goodbye to anyone.

We could have avoided the problems with Shauna if, as a group, we had discussed with compassion and understanding the place of children in our office setting. Creating a policy, or asking if one exists, deflects the attention from individuals and depersonalizes the situation to mean "children at work," not "Shauna at work." The insurance industry women agreed they would bring the women in their offices together to discuss feelings about children during the work day. Their purpose would be to establish guidelines that considered individual and group expectations.

No two offices will be the same. I know of a group of women in publishing who frequently work late into the evening. They established a system where workers' older children watched the younger ones in what they called their "giant work/playroom." I also know of a large realty office where the female realtors established a policy that said no children who were not actually working for their mothers could be in the building! In each case, the women had gotten together and agreed, openly, on a children-at-work policy.

For some women, creating a formal policy will not seem comfortable. In that case, polite consideration can also work to bring the children question out in the open and reduce tensions. If we are the ones with children, we can ask directly if it bothers our co-workers to have our children call after school or visit us during the work day. Then we must depersonalize the response and understand it applies to children in general, not just to our Susie or Tim, if a co-worker says she would appreciate calls and visits be kept to a minimum.

Betty's children do not call her during work unless they have an emergency. I, on the other hand, am a member of the 3 o'clock syndrome. When school's out, I want to touch base with my children. But I try to respect Betty's position. We have a small office and when the phone rings, either of us might answer. Instead of having my children call me and interrupt Betty, I wait for an appropriate time and call them, keeping the conversations short but satisfying my wish to have some contact with my kids during after-school hours.

As more women move into and up in the workplace, more children will be crossing the bridge between home and office. Many women and men welcome the humanizing effect that blending work and family can have on an otherwise harsh and product-focused environment. However, we need to respect that what warms our hearts may freeze someone else's. As a rule of thumb, in the workplace, work comes first. Work does not, though, have to exclude children. We bring our whole selves, our values and concerns about our families, with us to work. By talking openly about our expectations and respecting the limits of our co-workers' tolerance, we can come to a balance that acknowledges the workplace, our co-workers, ourselves, and our children.

Tamlin, a forty-year-old program manager who has no children, put the issue into perspective. "I like it when mothers and fathers bring their kids into the department. It gives me a chance to get an amplified picture, a sense of the whole person I can't see when all I know is what she does at work. I can appreciate some of the struggles and the joys of her life. Being a non-mother, I don't compare. I don't judge her. I observe and it helps me know her better. However, I don't want these visits to become a regular thing. Occasional contact with well-behaved children gentles the workplace. Anything that conflicts with getting the job done isn't acceptable."

Tamlin's assessment offers guidelines for all of us whose lives encompass both children and work. Working with women means working with their children. Confronting conflicts before they become problems requires tact, but can go a long way toward supporting women who value getting along with each other as a positive base for productive working relationships.

Suggestions for Getting Along

* Accept that you can learn to work with, appreciate, and even grow to like a woman whose style and manner conflict with your own. Follow the exercise in this chapter that asks you to identify her strengths and abilities. Acknowledging the value in different styles adds to our collective strength.

* Remember that all women do not share the same priorities in balancing our commitments to family, work, and the community. Each of us has a right to choose the balance that works best for us. Just as we want support for our choices, so do the women we work with need for us to respect their priorities. Whether I am concentrating all my time and energy on advancing in my career, or dividing my energy between my career and my family, what counts is how well I am performing the work I am responsible to contribute. Our competence and commitment to performance, not our personal priorities, should be the measure of our value at work.

* We love our children, but not everyone else welcomes intrusion from or about our children during working hours. Out of respect for your own needs and those of your co-workers, take the initiative in tactfully and openly discussing a children-and-work-policy in your office. Talk about after-school visits, covering for each other during emergencies and special events, and phone calls. Knowing other women's needs, expectations, and tolerance levels can help you work toward guidelines for children-and-work which everyone can accept and respect.

* If you would like more background on "Getting Along" issues, Barbara suggests you will find useful information in John Narciso and David Burkett's book *Declare Yourself: Discovering the Me in Relationships* (Spectrum Books, 1975) and *The Dance of Anger: A Women's Guide to Changing the Pattern of Intimate Relationships* by Harriet Goldhor Lerner, Ph.D. (Harper & Row, 1985).

10

Daughters, Mothers, and Mentors

She asks you to be more careful when reviewing the accounts; a more conscientious review would have picked up your error. You suddenly feel reduced, inadequate. You become defensive, retorting "Well, if you had told me what you wanted, I would have given it to you!" Your mother has suddenly appeared in the office, and you're back to being a little girl again, reacting emotionally to a woman who has no idea she's standing in for a ghost.

This mother stand-in did not choose her mother role. She doesn't know that what she has said or done has triggered for you a mother/daughter connection. However, many of us at some point in our working lives will find ourselves caught somewhere in a mother/daughter loop. Surprisingly, on our survey only fifteen women specifically referred to mother/daughter roles as problems for women. After approaching the subject directly with women, however, I believe many of us who find ourselves in conflict relationships should consider how those relationships may relate to our personal mother/daughter issues. After all, the mother/daughter relationship is fundamental in framing who we are and in teaching us how to conduct ourselves in the world. As daughters, we face the challenge of separating from our mothers and establishing an identity of our own. As mothers, we need to learn to let go of our children and the control we have had over their lives.

Much of what we bring from our experience as daughters and mothers can support us in the workplace. We have grown up with expectations of nurturing and caring that influence our positive relationships with other women. Many of us come from backgrounds where strong mothers have modeled belief in themselves and encouraged us to believe in ourselves. But when relationships in our past have not prepared us well to respond positively to women at work, our challenge is to take charge of ourselves and break the negative patterns that bind us in old, familiar patterns. In breaking destructive mother/daughter connections at work, we can discover our own identities and free other women to be themselves in positive and productive working relationships.

Working With Our Mothers

The emotional connections with our mothers go to the very marrow of our beings as women. For women, our relationship with our mothers is primary. Mother was the person who first offered us care and connection. She served as our role model. She molded us; we bear her imprint. However, while we are bound by our gender sameness, we need also to be separate, to be ourselves. As daughters, we struggle to detach ourselves from our mothers, even while we cherish the connection.

Men are not as bound by their attachment to their mothers. As a result, they operate more successfully on a functional level with their work associates. For women, however, conflicts or resentments associated with our mothers can make working for a woman who reminds us of her unproductive for everyone. "Women relating to each other see not just their friends or colleagues," write Louise Eichenbaum and Susie Orbach in *Between Women*, "they project onto them a whole range of emotions that reflect the legacy of their relationships with their mothers." It could be the way she answers the phone, or her way of telling us what needs to be done, or even her perfume that triggers the connection. How we react and how we feel sends us back to how we reacted and felt when we were little girls.

In her many years of therapy practice, Barbara has found that the original mother-daughter relationship frames the relationships a woman has and will have with other women the rest of her life. If our mother liked and trusted other women, she most likely trusted herself and liked us. From her we learned to expect positive feelings and trust from other women. On the other hand, if she felt that other women were critical of her, she may have been critical of herself and, consequently, critical of us as she projected onto us her insecurities. Those of us with a critical mother learned to expect criticism from other women and to doubt praise whenever they offer it.

In their book *Sisterhood Betrayed*, Jill Barber and Rita Watson confirm that regardless of whether our role models have been positive or negative, most daughters cannot leave their relationships with their mothers behind. "Research," they write, "tells us that, in general, women who leave their mothers feeling angry and emotionally unresolved usually find that they have a hard time coping in the workplace. They see other women as their mothers and rebel against them. By comparison, women who leave their mothers without separating from them emotionally have difficulty in the workplace because they are trying too hard to please their women bosses, and depend too much on the response they receive in return."

While not denying the potential problems, I feel Barber and Watson overemphasize the negative. I believe that for many of us, positive relationships with our mothers prepare us well for working with women. Many of us who come to work with a supportive mother behind us bring advantage to ourselves and our co-workers. We expect positive relationships with other women and we find them. And we give other women the benefit of the doubt when styles conflict or when they criticize our performance.

Karen Wilken, whose mother, Ester Peterson, received a Presidential Medal of Freedom in 1981 for her work as a consumer advocate, grew up observing a woman who modeled fierce commitment to her work. Peterson believed her daughter could be equally committed, competent, and fulfilled. When Karen first began working with women from her mother's generation, she assumed they all shared her mother's intensity and expectations for excellent performance. Karen welcomed criticism as a sign of respect and as necessary for professional development. Twenty-five years later, Karen still expects women she works with to be trustworthy, committed, and fulfilled by what they contribute. She accepts and offers positive criticism as a constructive way to develop talent and inform other women she cares.

Karen learned to trust other women, and to build her strengths on positive connections, from her mother. Unfortunately, not all women share Karen's experience. Some of our mothers prepared us to be watchful of women and insecure; other mothers were overbearing and constantly critical. When we find those mother figures in the workplace, it can have destructive consequences. Barbara frequently works with women trying to resolve often deep-seated issues with their mothers. For example, she says women with eating disorders often have boundary issues with an overbearing mother. They have not successfully separated themselves from their mothers and their mothers' expectations for them.

She cites her work with one woman, Myra, who was experiencing a recurrence of a bulimic binge and purge eating disorder she had battled throughout her teenage years. During one of her therapy sessions, Myra revealed that three months earlier a new manager, an older woman, had been hired at her office. The new woman wanted to know the details of how everyone worked and scheduled their time. She requested weekly updates on client files and barraged her staff with suggestions for improved efficiency and sales results. Myra felt targeted for extra scrutiny and reported to Barbara feelings of suffocation and being pushed around.

Barbara recognized a connection between Myra's invasive mother and the new manager. As a young girl, Myra had begun purging as an unconscious statement of independence. Her mother wanted to control Myra, but only Myra could control what she ate and retained. When the new manager appeared on the scene with a controlling manner, it sparked an old association in Myra's head, and she responded to this controlling behavior in a familiar way.

Making the connection between her response to her mother and her reaction to the manager helped Myra work toward resolving a complex set of issues surrounding Myra's individuation from her mother. Myra learned to keep her boss's demands on a business level, not a personal one, and her purging stopped as she gained control of her boundaries. For Myra, the encounter with a mother figure at work actually resulted in a resolution of old issues and progress toward healthy adult growth.

Sometimes a painful issue with a mother remains hidden until a person at work makes us take a closer look at our responses. This happened to Jeannene, and she went to Barbara to try to understand her actions.

Jeannene, the mother of two children and the wife of a successful businessman, went back to school to finish a master's degree in industrial engineering. She received more than five job offers, but she didn't take the best offer because her boss would have been a woman. By refusing the best offer, she settled on $8,000 a year less, which didn't make sense financially. It did make sense, however, in a psychological way, given what Jeannene's mother had modeled for her about women.

Jeannene is an incest survivor, and her mother had known what was going on. Instead of protecting Jeannene by confronting the perpetrator or seeking intervention, her mother had allowed the abuse to happen. As a result, Jeannene learned not to trust women. She learned not to count on them for support or protection. She expected that a woman would sacrifice another woman to protect her own position, as her mother had sacrificed Jeannene to protect her husband and their relationship. Therefore, when Jeannene was faced with the prospect of a female boss, someone she would have to trust to deal fairly, she couldn't accept the risk.

Understanding the connection between her mother and her inability to trust women gave Jeannene a useful tool for approaching her relationships with other women, especially women in authority and older women. She began to try to trust others and learned to delegate important tasks, though at first depending on other women was difficult. She began working with women in higher positions than her own and grew to respect their abilities and their willingness to provide help and support. With Barbara's help, she learned to confront her childhood experiences and control her responses to other women.

Jeannene took an important step when she recognized her problem with working for a woman and sought Barbara's help. There are other women, though, who may retreat to open or often secretive use of alcohol or drugs to calm their heightened anxieties. According to Barbara, projections by the National Council on Alcoholism and Drug Dependency estimate women will spend $30 billion on alcohol by 1994, a $10 billion increase from 1984. "Such alternative coping styles can affect the woman's work behavior and performance," Barbara says, "and might trigger negative responses from female co-workers, especially those who are adult children of alcoholics."

Of course, not every woman will seek therapy or resort to alcohol or drugs when another woman triggers an emotional mother/daughter response. If you recognize any of your mother/daughter patterns in your reactions with other women, perhaps reviewing and questioning your relationship with your mother might provide some insights. For me, realizing that my first supervisor had triggered associations with my mother led me to a new understanding of my relationship with my mother and to a better way to respond to women at work. I was able to separate my emotional responses from my rational ones; as a result, I benefitted from working with an outstanding woman.

When I first started teaching at Pennsbury High School in Pennsylvania, my curriculum supervisor, Joyce, made frequent visits to my classroom. Joyce was as lavish with criticism as she was with praise and enthusiasm. She offered suggestions and judgements on everything from the clothes I wore to how I had presented a lesson on *The Scarlet Letter*.

I did not respond well to Joyce's attempts at encouraging my professional development. Rather, I interpreted her comments as assertions of her superiority and criticism of my "know-nothingness." Whenever she entered the door of my

English class, I felt myself shrink, trying to hide from whatever I was about to do wrong. As soon as she left, my sigh of relief restored my stature. Immediately and defiantly, I readjusted the window shade she had just lowered. If she had scowled at a point I had made about Hester Pryne, I expounded on that point. If Joyce had stopped by a student's desk to note his incomplete assignment, I created an excuse for him and then gave the whole class an extra day to turn in their work!

One night when I was complaining about Joyce, my husband looked up from his book and asked, "Are you talking about Joyce or your mother?" The light dawned. I had not made the connection between the two women earlier because physically and stylistically, my mother and Joyce came from different molds. However, I was reacting to another woman's professional attention as I had reacted as a teenager to my mother's personal criticism. I felt smothered by a woman who I thought wanted to control me rather than serve as a mentor. I realized that my unconscious assumptions were inventing conflicts where only good intentions existed. As with other women who have associated coworkers with their mothers, I was holding a good woman liable for wrongs of which she was innocent!

Literally the next day, I approached Joyce with a new attitude. I accepted her intentions as professionally motivated. I welcomed her critiques and benefitted from opportunities to participate in her seminars and workshops. I chose to see Joyce for who she was, and she became an important role model for me as I advanced through my teaching career.

The woman who reminds you of your mother need not be old enough to be your mother. Anyone who makes us feel as if we are with our mothers can fill the role. No matter who she is, however, it is up to us to break the connection. First, we must learn to ask ourselves whether a negative response to a woman at work might be because she reminds us of our mother. If she does, we must then ask ourselves if our responses to her remind us of the behaviors we used with our mother. Finally, if those behaviors do not serve us well in our offices or our careers, we can choose to stop them. We can tell ourselves that the woman standing before us is not our mother. We can remind ourselves that we are adults and that the women we interact with are adults. We can approach this woman who reminds us of our mother with a fresh perspective and a positive, depersonalized receptivity to what she can offer.

If you find yourself reacting to a mother figure at work, the tools suggested in the "Taking It Personally" chapter can help. Learning to separate how we feel about our mothers from how we choose to react to negative workplace "mothers" helps us to depersonalize an emotional connection and return to productive work. We will be free to develop our independent adult selves, modeled on who we choose to be. And the women who remind us of our mothers will no longer be frustrated by trying to work through reactions they don't have the insight to understand.

The following exercise has helped women break free from destructive mother/daughter patterns at work. If you find yourself in a similar situation, perhaps this process can help you too:

First, identify what it is that triggers your mother/daughter response. Is it the way this woman tells you to do something? Is it the attitude she displays toward other people? Is it the words she uses to criticize your performance or suggest improvement? Is it the way she tries to protect or take care of you?

Next, try to remember how you felt when your mother behaved that way. Ask yourself if you feel the same way with this other woman. Then ask yourself if you are reacting today with this woman at work the same way you reacted (or still react) to your mother.

Now ask yourself if the way you are reacting seems positive, mature, and constructive. If not, if you recognize that you are caught in the old destructive patterns, decide that you will STOP behaving that way and break the pattern. CHOOSE a more mature and productive way to respond to this woman who reminds you of your mother. Say out loud to yourself, "When _____ does or says _____ again, I CHOOSE to respond by _____." The control you will gain by choosing your response will be both exhilarating and empowering.

The sensitive issue of mother/daughter relationship is not always easy to identify or resolve. However, stepping back and looking at our situation from a humorous perspective can help us objectify our relationship and gain helpful insights. The cartoon strip "CATHY," for example, often presents the mother/daughter relationship with understanding humor. Seeing our fears and foibles handled lightly but with compassion may provide us a first step toward objectifying our relationship with our mothers and approaching healthy resolution of our mother/daughter issues.

When We Mother Other Women

Some women go to work and find their "mothers." Other women, consciously or unconsciously, bring their mother persona to work and find "daughters" with whom to act out their parts. Their intentions may reflect positive, nurturing values, but in a workplace context their actions and assumptions can frustrate, even anger, those they deem part of their schemes. These women tend to play the part of "hover-mother," taking care of their "daughters" by shielding them from failure or sacrificing themselves to ease the pressure on their striving co-workers.

For some women, making the transition from the home environment to a work environment can be difficult. Women who act as mothers can have a tendency to over-nurture coworkers and to come across as overbearing, overinvolved and a nag. During one workshop I was conducting, a woman who introduced herself as Corinna made this comment: "I am used to being the boss, not being bossed. Perhaps those of us who were wives and mothers before being in the work force have a special problem to overcome in working with others."

Barbara agrees that needing to mother often can be a problem for women, especially when the mother role has been central to their identity or when they have never had a chance to play out the part. "Women who identify primarily with their roles as mothers often cannot separate from that role at work," Barbara says. "But they don't have to be mothers to base their esteem on functioning as caretakers, nurturers, givers." Women who go home to lonely, sometimes desperate situations might view work as the only place where they feel they can create the nurturing connections they need.

These "mothering" women can become the office caretakers, watching out for everyone's needs, from extra support during rush periods to advice on cold remedies. They make themselves indispensable, taking over control of the coffee closet and information on everything from client backgrounds to suppliers and vendors. They tend to wear themselves to exhaustion presenting themselves as saviors and working extra hours to ease the pressure on others.

Mothering women do more than pull their own weight, and they make sure others recognize their sacrifice. They need to be needed, and they need to know, even if they have to say so aloud themselves, that the office "couldn't have gotten through that one" without them.

Often it becomes the responsibility of a specific woman

to interrupt the mothering woman's behaviors and to help her recognize the often suffocating effect she has on her co-workers. Too often other women accept the attentions of a mother without appreciating that so much giving leaves little of a woman for herself, whether it be energy or esteem. A co-worker or manager can help a workplace mother realize that people do appreciate her work and that she needs to let others share in the responsibilities she has taken on.

If you manage a mother type, be specific in reminding her of her work-related role. Satisfy her need to be needed by connecting her job to the department or company goals. Lead her to appreciate how women can help others most by encouraging them to take on challenges. As a reward for letting others complete their own projects and leaving work at a reasonable hour, reward her with what she values most: knowing people appreciate her. Invite her to lunch and say thank you; then go back to work!

Not all mothers at work come ready to sacrifice and nurture. Some see their roles as controllers, manipulating the workplace with their judgmental attitudes, coming to work to punish daughters who have rejected or abandoned them. Darla attended one of our workshops and shared the following experience. Darla, twenty-eight, supervised Hannah, whose daughter, Darla told us, had left home at nineteen and refused any communication with her mother. Hannah saw Darla and other young women in their lab as ungrateful daughters who considered themselves superior to their older mother. When Darla would suggest changes in a recording method, Hannah would find a way to turn the situation around and lecture Darla on her "lousy" supervisory skills or the "mess of a desk that will get you in trouble one day."

Hannah intimidated Darla, but Darla knew she could not let Hannah use her or other women as substitute daugh-ters. It seemed possible that Hannah, wounded by her daughter and angry at having to work for a woman her daughter's age, probably felt worthless and abandoned. Though Darla anticipated no easy cure for Hannah's hurt feelings, she determined to depersonalize her reactions to Hannah's criticisms and to help build Hannah's esteem. Darla realized Hannah knew details about the lab operation Darla had yet to learn. She decided to ask Hannah to bring her up to speed on lab operations to help her improve her supervisory skills. Hannah didn't want to be a supervisor herself, but she had observed other supervisors and was willing to share her experience.

I met Darla a month later. Redirecting Hannah's mothering needs from punishing Darla to helping her succeed had made a positive difference. Hannah wasn't criticizing Darla, and she seemed pleased that a younger women could find value in what she had to contribute. The other women in the lab reported that Hannah seemed less critical of them, too, and occasionally offered them positive advice instead of negative criticism. Looking at Hannah's behaviors objectively and planning a constructive response has helped Darla and the other women in her lab work more comfortably and productively with a difficult workplace mother.

Hannah wanted to punish daughters she found at work. Other women want to gain control of their groups and organizations. Nina, a woman in her mid-forties, has manipulated control of her development team by positioning herself as an essential caretaker. She feels if she isn't in control and at the center, others might not notice her contributions and consider her superfluous. For Nina, mothering means knowing it all and having absolute control. She awaits any opportunity to rescue her colleagues, and then jumps in with zeal to prove how she can fix everything and make it better. She gains control of information and apportions it out according to who has been good (to her) and who must be sent to bed without any supper.

With a "mother" like Nina, solutions require strong measures. The daughters in her group must not shrink under Nina's attempts at control. They must thank Nina for her offers to assist, insist on rescuing themselves, and demand the information they need, not wait to have it rewarded. And they must let her know that they all have a stake in the team's success. Nina's need to control fosters dependence on a central figure, the mother, and works against the goal of good team function. If Nina would concentrate on the talent she contributes instead of the control she needs, the whole group can succeed; and they will thank Nina for her part!

Mothers like Nina come tough; it takes tough women to stand up and say, "You can't play that game here." If we see her coming and we don't take action, we have no one to blame but ourselves.

Not all workplace mothers act out their inclinations in the broader workplace arena. Often a mother selects one specific "daughter" and showers—or drowns—her with misplaced nurture and protection. Donna worked with such a woman. Mrs. Crandall, old enough to be Donna's mother, saw Donna as the "daughter she never had." Mrs. Crandall arranged opportunities for Donna to go on buying trips to other cities and nudged her, with pride, into situations for which Donna had neither the preparation nor the job title to qualify. When Donna faltered, Mrs. Crandall made excuses and covered for her. Mrs. Crandall worried over Donna's single lifestyle and invited her for Sunday dinners, weekend trips, and family birthdays.

Soon Donna realized that she was trapped into acting like a daughter when what she wanted was to learn a job and build a career! She tried to withdraw from Mrs. Crandall; but every time she said, "No thank you" to a sales meeting or a Sunday barbecue, Mrs. Crandall became hurt and Donna felt guilty. The minute an opening became available at another store, Donna leapt at the opportunity to transfer. Mrs Crandall confronted her saying, "How can you leave me like this? After all I have done for you! No one else will take care of you like I have!"

Donna assures me now that she will never again let a mother like Mrs. Crandall take care of her at all! She figures she lost an important year by being protected when she could have been making mistakes and learning as she went. If she had stayed at Mrs. Crandall's and had found herself in a position to compete with Mrs. Crandall for a management position, she would have had to deal with competing with a mother. Consciously or unconsciously, mothers who claim daughters may also be protecting themselves from having the daughters compete with them.

Competition between women can be difficult enough, but adding the emotional dimension of a daughter competing with a mother pulls at the roots of mother-daughter connections. While, in fact, daughters compete with mothers in every area from looks to popularity to career success, we are uncomfortable with that reality. Laura Tracy, author of *Secrets Between Us: Women and Competition*, notes, "While in her gut a daughter knows that she's in competition with her mother, she is told covertly that surpassing her mother can be very dangerous. . . . Unlike sons, who are encouraged, however indirectly, to challenge and compete with fathers in order to become adult men, daughters are discouraged from challenging their mothers."

And, Barbara adds, it is often the mothers themselves who discourage the competition. On one level, of course we want our daughters to succeed. But on another level, our roles have not prepared us for our daughters to surpass us. This conflict creates a challenge in any mother/daughter relationship, within the family or in a workplace context.

Marilyn, a psychologist and professor, assumed the role of mother with Mary Jo, an outstanding student she first met in one of her seminars. They conducted research together and Marilyn integrated Mary Jo into her family of grown children. Marilyn was always the professional guide but she became more often a caring mother. She nursed Mary Jo through health problems and worried about her relationships. When Marilyn retired, the university offered her position to Mary Jo. While she expected to feel honored that her favorite student was filling her open position, Marilyn instead was surprised to feel a surge of competitive anger, even jealousy, that her "daughter" had already matched her accomplishments and was likely to surpass her!

When Mary Jo called to share her excitement and suggest they celebrate together, the issue came into focus for Marilyn. She realized that she had given this surrogate daughter what every mother wants to give: support and encouragement to help her achieve her best. Marilyn also realized she felt a sadness because she would no longer be in the position of active guide, of providing the example. However, she could still offer Mary Jo advice, based on her experience and on her continuing professional interest. She also realized that Mary Jo's faculty appointment represented Marilyn's own goals for Mary Jo and that Mary Jo's success was a compliment to their relationship, not a challenge.

Marilyn shared with Mary Jo the moment of pain that turned to pride. Her advice to Mary Jo was "encourage your students. Care about them and support them, but don't confuse your professional association with a mother/daughter relationship. The emotions can inhibit both of you when you face competitive issues. Instead, encourage your protege to develop her skills and her independence. Then enjoy watching her succeed!"

I'm *Not* Your Mother!

Some women want to be mother at work. Many others, however, emphatically do not! When they come to work, they leave their aprons and care-taking tendencies at home. They approach their work associates as co-contributors and they resent assumptions that because they may look old enough to be someone's mother, they also have to play the part!

One woman told a workshop exactly how she felt: "I'm fifty-one," she said, "and I've worked hard to get where I am. Often I find myself having to remind younger women, and even some men, that I am not their mother! They whine to me or want me to take care of their problems. I don't have time to play mother when I have a division to run."

Most women don't want to be cast as mother at work. The intricacies and complications of such a relationship threatens productive, business-focused work. The daughter often makes the identification without any complicity from the mother. She brings with her all the baggage from her childhood and dumps it onto the unsuspecting woman's desk, expecting this woman to somehow understand the expectations and emotions involved.

When we find ourselves cast in the mother role against our wishes, we must be willing to firmly break the connection. Pat, a manager at a pharmaceutical company, often discovers herself cast as a mother. When one of her staff members, a woman young enough to be Pat's daughter, began pouting and otherwise reacting in a more adolescent than adult manner, Pat addressed the situation directly.

"I told her I thought she was behaving as though I was her mother. I assured her I was not. I emphasized that I was her manager and that we had work to do together. I told her I expected the quality performance from her that I expected from all my staff. If a report required a revision, I meant the report wasn't good enough, not that she wasn't good enough. I told her our ages made no difference, but our responsibilities to each other did. I made it clear she was to expect no special favors or consideration. She cried and asked why I was being 'so mean' to her. I responded that I valued her skills and saw she had good potential. I wasn't being mean— I was doing her a favor by telling her not to expect mothering. Eventually the emotions subsided and we now have a clean, appropriate workplace relationship."

Pat did herself and the young woman a service by being direct and honest. She broke the mother connection and cleared the air for a different, more professional and more productive relationship.

From Mothers to Mentors

"I don't need another mother," Kristen, a young systems integrator with Andersen Consulting, told me. "I have a great, supportive mother at home. I'm at work, and I want a mentor." Kristen refers to an important distinction that women need to recognize—a good mother nurtures; a mentor empowers.

Empowering means to enable, to authorize, to give power to. When we empower other women, we give them the tools and the permission to succeed on their own. We empower by delegating tasks that encourage women to take responsibility and to learn to act independently. Unlike some nurturers who protect others from risk, empowerers support women in taking risks. We believe challenge is the best teacher. When we nurture, we say, "I will help make you ready." When we empower, we say, "You are ready; you can."

The source for nurturing comes from our need to care, from our wanting to feed and protect others. The mother/daughter bond, with all its emotional complications, is not always conducive to self-definition and independence. Our source for mentoring, however, comes from our work experience. Mentors are committed to developing other women into capable and independent performers. Mentors know how to succeed at work. They pass on what they have learned to the women they select for their attention and guidance.

Good mentoring relationships are reciprocal: the woman receiving guidance from a sponsor responds with support for her mentor. She brings new information for review and carries her mentor's ideas to subordinates and others in the organization. Mentors and those they mentor depend on each other, but in a positive and healthy way.

Mentors are not mothers. They are not friends. They many not even be work friends. Mentors do not have to like us personally to respect us and recognize our potential. Mentors are role models, women who acknowledge the value of an often younger woman and agree to serve as her guide, counselor, coach, and advocate. They provide information, criticism, and opportunity. The woman Kristen wants to find would provide an example of what women can accomplish. She would also share what she knows and, in return, she would be assured that a capable young woman will follow in her path as a talented contributor to her company's future.

Jacqueline, a woman who considers herself a mentor within her organization, describes why young women seek her guidance. "I am perceived as a person with power and responsibility," Jacqueline says. "My experience has taught me that women want to work for women who are considered important and successful. It gives them status—and example. I model the type of woman they want to become."

In the January 1988 issue of *Savvy* magazine, Anne B. Fisher referenced a study of female senior executives from large U.S. companies. Seventy-eight percent of these women said they were serving as mentors, actively helping women under them to move up. Though women I talk with frequently lament that no formal structure exists for mentoring in their workplaces, most confirm that some informal sort of mentoring has helped them or women they know. The advantage of a formal system, they say, is that openly acknowledged mentor/mentee relationships would eliminate some of the complications and conflicts associated with friendship or mother/daughter relationships. Institutionalizing the system would give mentoring both respectability and durability.

"It is difficult to institutionalize mentoring programs, but it has been done," writes Felice Schwartz of the Catalyst research organization. "Corning, among other companies, has found that mentoring is making a difference in its ability to promote and retain women." Though she acknowledges that men can certainly mentor women, Schwartz adds that "a woman is probably still a better role model for a woman." Many women take their informal roles as mentors seriously and give generously of their time and experience. We interact with women at work, on boards and committees, and in professional groups and organizations. We share ideas with women who seek us out because we have succeeded at what they wish to try. In our visible position as women entrepreneurs, my partner and I are often approached by women who want to know "how we did it." We answer their questions and invite them to stay in touch as they enter their new ventures. We thank the women who offered us their time and expertise when we were just beginning. And we believe we have a responsibility to follow their model and support the women who can learn from us.

Whether institutionalized or informal, mentoring provides a way for women to encourage and develop other women whom they find dedicated, motivated, and talented.

Mentors for the future will model and advise not only on how to operate within the organization but also how to balance commitment priorities within and without the workplace. As the workplace becomes more flexible and women manage our careers in accordance with our family, work, and community priorities, we will need mentors to show us the way. We will select mentors who model the whole life we want to experience and the whole person we want to become. Mentoring gives women a new and positive way to connect with other women and to demonstrate that we care about each other and about our future.

Suggestions to Manage "Mother/Daughter" Work Relationships

* As women in the workplace, we must learn to separate our reactions to our mothers from our responses to women at work who remind us of our mothers. Mother/daughter relationships are complex and affect us profoundly. If you believe you have unresolved issues with your mother that are affecting your work relationships, you might want to work with a trained therapist who can guide you toward understanding. The following books may also give you insight and support: *The Courage to Heal: A Guide for Women Survivors of Child Abuse* by Ellen Bass (HarperCollins Publishers, Inc., 1992); *It Will Never Happen to Me* by Claudia Black (Ballantine Books, 1981); *Bradshaw on the Family: A Revolutionary Way to Self-Discovery* by John Bradshaw (Health Communications, Inc., 1988); *How to Manage Your Mother: Skills and Strategies to Improve Mother-Daughter Relationships* by Nancy Wasserman Cocola and Arlene Modica Matthews (Simon & Schuster, 1992); *Women and Substance Use* by Elizabeth Ettorre (Rutgers University Press, 1992); *Toxic Parents: Overcoming Their Hurtful*

Legacy & Reclaiming Your Life by Dr. Susan Forward (Bantam Books, 1989); *Family Constellation* by Walter Toman (Springer Publishing Co., 1992).

  * As mothers coming to work, we must respect that other women have a right to their independence, their successes and failures. On the job we must interact with other women as equals in exercising our job functions. We may be mothers at home, but we are co-workers in the office.

  * Women need mentors. If you are just beginning or continuing to build your career, get to know women you admire at work, in the community, on boards or committees. Invite them for coffee. Find out what they are doing and how they have achieved their success. Don't forget to let them know you appreciate their time and information! Seek out a particular woman who models what you want to achieve. If you feel comfortable approaching her and asking for her coaching and guidance, by all means do. She will most likely accept your invitation to mentor as a compliment. Remember, however, that conscientious mentoring takes time; respect that her first responsibility is to her own job and career. Also remember that a mentoring relationship is reciprocal. She helps you and you support her with information and positive networking.

  * Become a mentor yourself. If your workplace sponsors a formal mentoring program, volunteer to participate. If you know other women who have served as mentors, learn how they arranged their time and what opportunities and information they offered their mentees. When you identify a woman you would like to mentor, make sure both you and she understand that this is a career-focused, coaching relationship, not a mother/daughter relationship and not a personal friendship (though certainly you may like and be friendly with each other!)

The
Future
is
Ours

11

Women
Will
Lead

Over the past twenty years women have struggled in the workplace to prove our abilities and our dedication, our skills and our talents. Fortunately, we have succeeded to a large measure. The business world has grown to appreciate our good work and to respect our feminine values and culture. Now women have an extraordinary opportunity to model for the workplace a balance of relationship values and productivity that will lead us into the 21st century.

Today, the workplace more and more assigns teams of workers to make decisions that affect products and policies. These teams function like communities. Building effective teams depends on our being able to establish comfortable, productive relationships where individuals cooperate for a mutual benefit. Female leadership style tends to enhance community. It strives to be inclusive, sharing information and responsibility, rather than exclusive, reserving authority for a select few.

Juanita Brown, president of Whole Systems Associates, an international consortium dedicated to strategic change
in management, sees these images of community emerging
as people describe corporations for the future. As part of her
research, she asked both senior executives and line personnel
from the United States and other countries to describe their
images of "corporation" and "community." "Consistently,"
Brown writes in *New Traditions in Business*, "'Corporation'
conjures up images of authority, bureaucracy, competition,
power, and profit. 'Community' consistently evokes images
of democracy, diversity, cooperation, interdependence, and
mutual benefit." The images people associate with community could also be used to describe the values of our female
culture, a culture that has already begun to transform the
American workplace.

A leading futurist, Willis Harman, Ph.D., in his essay
"21st Century Business: A Background for Dialogue," identifies the women's movement as seminal to fundamental and
necessary changes in American business. "Among the many
social phenomena that convey and denote the shifting values
emphasis, one particular transition stands out—the women's
movement. Beyond being a movement of women, asserting
women's rights, it stresses the benefits and importance of a
feminine point of view for all humans. All of us possess
masculine and feminine characteristics. The feminine focus
involves an emphasis on such values as caring, nurturing,
cooperating, and creating. It focuses on a perception of
relationships rather than things, of wholeness over parts, and
the authenticity of inner knowing. It relates to the liberation
of the feminine energies in the male as well as the female."

The movement away from male corporate values and
toward female community values for tomorrow's workplace
reflects the "shifting values emphasis" Harman describes in
his essay. As we emerge from a corporate mentality and enter

the new workplace community, women will lead the way.

Women are prepared to lead the transition from a corporate workplace to a community workplace because we have learned how to function in a community culture. We have the opportunity to lead because we have recently accomplished a "critical mass" based on our numbers and our positions within the workplace. According to the authors of *Megatrends for Women*, women today "are poised to win top leadership posts in both the corporate culture and independently-owned small- to mid-size businesses. But they will not do so as carbon copies of the businessmen they follow—they bring with them their own leadership style hammered out and tested over the years. But that leadership will also be tempered by the call of balance, family, and recreation."

Balance is the pivotal concept for the future. How we balance personal needs with the practical demands of a functioning workplace community and our own career goals will determine our job satisfaction and our credibility as models for the new system. The flexible workplace, recognized by Felice Schwartz and others as essential to attracting and retaining women in the future, respects that women and men will have changing commitment priorities throughout our working years. Within the flexible workplace we can plan our careers to achieve a balance between personal needs and career commitment.

To make the best decisions for ourselves and for our careers, we will be expected to know ourselves and to respect our needs as whole people. We will also recognize and respect the people we work with as whole people who are balancing their own personal priorities and career goals. Caring for the whole person, an important value in the female culture, now has value in the workplace as well. How we acknowledge others and express our support and caring will become a model for the new workplace.

As the workplace evolves toward community values, our organizations are undergoing other changes as well. Corporations in the future will have fewer middle level managers, and fewer executive positions at the top. We will no longer be able to rely on salary increases and titles to reward our performance efforts. The quality of our workplace relationships will significantly influence our job satisfaction. The caring and sensitivity we bring to work will create strong bonds to hold together our workplace communities and to give us the satisfaction we demand. However, we must learn to balance our sensitivity and emotionally-based behaviors with a cooperative commitment to performance and productivity.

Women have always valued cooperation. When we recognize that by managing our behaviors we contribute to a positive working environment for everyone, we will want to cooperate. Mutual caring means mutual benefits. Those who care will be those who lead.

JoAnne Van Etten, a systems analyst who has been with Guilford Transportation Industries for twenty years, feels passionately about our future. "Women care about the broad scheme of integrity and order in their lives. For the future, we need to know that we can be effective at the middle as well as the upper levels of management, and we need to appreciate that we are good at what we do. Our greatest opportunity is that we can choose what we want to be. Without holistic goals for ourselves, we will find only emptiness in our careers and in our lives as our careers end."

As women, we need to learn from one another how to attain a satisfying balance in our lives. Women need for each other to continue as mentors even as we model for others what we have already learned about working in a relationship-based community. Women in corporations, in schools, in hospitals, in laboratories, and publication offices are coming together to talk about their lives. These women already value who they are both as women and as contributors to their corporations and professions. What they talk about are concerns over balancing their lives and making choices. These women share information about career opportunities and workplace organization, and they also talk about how they manage their personal and work priorities. They respect each other as being committed, dedicated, and competent, and they learn from one another how to be more effective at work and in their personal lives.

"While the women's movement was primarily about jobs, choices, and money, it was also about women networking with women," Jill Barber and Rita Watson write in *Sisterhood Betrayed*. "An important goal for women is to come up with some sort of networking equivalent to the old-boy system that has held women back for so long. We need to create an old-girl system whereby women will help women." The old-boy networks of our society still function, especially in traditional corporations where the impact of the female style has yet to initiate change. Whether that old-boy system continues to hold us back in the new workplace depends on how strong an old-girl system we can create.

Women, proud of who we are, must reach out to other women and share what we have learned about balance. We must mentor younger women and let ourselves be mentored by older women. Finally, we must willingly accept the responsibility we have earned to lead the workplace from corporation to community. Women working with women have learned to be our best together. From our example will come the future.

Bibliography

Patricia Aburdene and John Naisbitt. *Megatrends for Women*. Villard Books, 1992.

Jill Barber. *Sisterhood Betrayed*. St. Martin's Press, 1991.

Ellen Bass. *The Courage to Heal: A Guide for Women Survivors of Child Abuse*. HarperCollins Publishers, Inc., 1992.

Mary Catherine Bateson. *Composing a Life*. Penguin Books, 1990.

Paula Bernstein. *Family Ties, Corporate Bond*. Doubleday, 1985.

Claudia Black. *It Will Never Happen to Me*. Ballantine Books, 1981.

Joseph H. Boyett and Henry P. Conn. *Workplace 2000: The Revolution Reshaping American Business*. Penguin Books, 1991.

John Bradshaw. *Bradshaw on the Family: A Revolutionary Way to Self-Discovery*. Health Communications, Inc., 1988.

Judith Briles. *The Confidence Factor*. Master Media Limited, 1990.

_____. *Woman to Woman: From Sabotage to Success*. New Horizon Press, 1987.

Jerry Brinegar. *Breaking Free from Domestic Violence*. CompCare Publishers, 1992.

Nancy Wasserman Cocola and Arlene Modica Matthews. *How to Manage Your Mother: Skills and Strategies to Improve Mother-Daughter Relationships*. Simon & Schuster, 1992.

Colette Dowling. *Perfect Women*. Summit Books, 1988.

Louise Eichenbaum and Susie Orbach. *Between Women*. Viking Penguin, Inc., 1988.

_____. *What Do Women Want, Exploding the Myth of Dependency*. Berkeley Books, 1983.

Cynthia Fuchs Epstein. *Deceptive Distinctions*. Yale University Press, 1990.

Shelley Espinosa. *Working Solutions from Working Secretaries*. Kendall/Hunt, 1987.

Elizabeth Ettorre. *Women and Substance Use*. Rutgers University Press, 1992.

Cris Evatt. *Opposite Sides of the Bed: A Lively Guide to the Differences between Women and Men*. Conari Press, 1993.

Susan Faludi. *Backlash: The Undeclared War Against American Women*. Crown Publishers, 1991.

Jaclyn Fierman. "Do Women Manage Differently?" *Fortune*, December 17, 1990.

Anne B. Fisher. "When Will Women Get to the Top." *Fortune*, September 21, 1992.

_____. "Dirty Little Secrets." *Savvy*, January 1988.

Dr. Susan Forward. *Betrayal of Innocence: Incest and Its Devastation*. Penguin Books, 1979.

_____. *Toxic Parents: Overcoming Their Hurtful Legacy and Reclaiming Your Life*. Bantam Books, 1989.

Dr. Arthur Freeman and Rose DeWolf. *Woulda, Coulda, Shoulda: Overcoming Regrets, Mistakes, and Missed Opportunities*. William Morrow, 1989.

Marilyn French. *Beyond Power: On Women, Men, and Morals*. Ballantine Books, 1985.

Nancy Friday. *Jealousy*. Bantam Books, 1985.

_____. *My Mother/Myself*. Delacorte, 1977.

Dennis A. Gilbert. *The Compendium of American Public Opinion*, 1988.

Carol Gilligan. *In a Different Voice*. Harvard University Press, 1982.

Jon Gueijo. "Jealousy and Envy: The Demons within Us." *Bostonia*. May/June 1988.

John Gray, Ph.D. *Men, Women, and Relationship*. Beyond Words Publishing, Inc., 1988.

_____. *Men are from Mars, Women are from Venus*. HarperCollins Publishers, 1992.

Christian Hageseth. *A Laughing Place*. Berwick Publishing Company, 1988.

Sarah Hardesty and Nehama Jacobs. *Success and Betrayal: The Crisis of Women in Corporate America*. Franklin Watts, 1986.

Sally Helgesen. *The Female Advantage: Women's Ways of Leadership*. Doubleday, 1990.

Arlie Hochschild. *Second Shift*. Viking, 1989.

Linda A. Hughes. "But That's Not (Really) Mean: Competing in a Cooperative Mode." *Sex Roles: A Journal of Research*. *19*(11-12), 1988.

Dorothy Jongeward and Dru Scott. *Women as Winners*. Addison-Wesley Publishing Co., 1983.

Julia Kagan. "Survey: Work in the 1980's and 1990's." *Working Woman*, April 1983.

Rosabeth Moss Kanter. *Men and Women of the Corporation*. Basic Books, 1977.

Anne Katherine, MA. *Where You End and I Begin*. Parkside Publishing Co., 1991.

Alfie Kohn. *No Contest: The Case Against Competition*. Revised Edition. Houghton Mifflin Company, 1992.

Robin Tolmach Lakoff. *Talking Power: The Politics of Language*. Basic Books, 1990.

Elinor Lenz and Barbara Myenhoff. *The Feminization of America*. Jeremy P. Tancher, Inc., 1985.

Harriet Goldhor Lerner, Ph.D. *The Dance of Anger: A Woman's Guide to Changing the Pattern of Relationships*. Harper & Row, 1985.

Lloyd S. Lewan. *Women in the Workplace: A Man's Perspective*. Remington Press, 1988.

Elizabeth L'Hommedieu. "Walking Out on the Boys." *Time*, July 8, 1991.

Marilyn Loden. *Feminine Leadership or How to Succeed in Business Without Being One of the Boys*. Random House, Inc., 1985.

Tara Roth Madden. *Women vs Women: The Uncivil Business War*. AMACOM, 1987.

Nicky Marone. *Women and Risk: A Guide to Overcoming Learned Helplessness*. St. Martin's Press, 1992.

Jinx Melia and Pauline Lyttle. *Why Jenny Can't Lead*. Operational Politics, Inc., 1986.

Jean Baker Miller, M.D. *Toward a New Psychology of Women*. Beacon Press, 1976.

John Narciso and David Burkett. *Declare Yourself: Discovering the Me in Relationships*. Spectrum Books, 1975.

Anne Moir and David Jessel. *Brain Sex: The Real Difference Between Men and Women*. Lyle Stuart, 1991.

Ann M. Morrison, Randall P. White, and Ellen Van Velsorand. *Breaking the Glass Ceiling*. The Center for Creative Leadership, Addison-Wesley Publishing Co., 1987.

Sharon Nelton. "Men, Women and Leadership." *Nation's Business*. May, 1991.

Tom Peters. "The Best New Managers Will Listen, Motivate, Support. Isn't That Just Like a Woman." *Working Woman*. September 1990.

Renesch, John (Ed.) "21st-Century Business: A Background for Dialogue." *New Traditions in Business: Spirit and Leadership in the 21st Century*. Berrett-Kochler Publishers, San Francisco, 1992.

Judy Rosener. "How Women Lead." *Harvard Business Review*, November-December, 1990.

_____ and Marilyn Loden. *Workforce America*. Dow Jones Irwin, 1991.

Alice G. Sargent. *The Androgynous Manager*. AMACOM, 1983.

Anne Wilson Schaef. *Women's Reality*. Winston Press, 1981.

Dr. Adele Scheele. "You're Jealous. What Career Envy Really Means." *Working Woman*, September 1991.

_____. "Learning to Compete With Women." *Working Woman*. November 1992.

Felice N. Schwartz. *Breaking With Tradition*. Warner Books, 1992.

Jeannette R. Scollard. *The Self-Employed Woman: How to Start Your Own Business and Gain Control of Your Life*. Simon & Schuster, Inc., 1985.

Joan Shapiro, M.D. *Men: A Translation for Women*. Penguin Books, USA, Inc., 1992.

Gloria Steinem. *Revolution From Within: A Book of Self-Esteem*. Little, Brown and Company, 1992.

Deborah Tannen, Ph.D. *You Just Don't Understand: Men and Women in Conversation*. William Morrow, 1990.

_____. "How to Close the Communication Gap Between Men and Women." *McCall's*, May 1991.

Carol Tavris. *The Mismeasure of Women*. Simon & Schuster, 1992.

Ann McKay Thompson and Marcia Donnan Wood. *Management Strategies for Women*. Simon & Schuster, 1980.

Walter Toman. *Family Constellation*. Springer Publishing Co., 1992.

Laura Tracy. *Secrets Between Us: Women and Competition*, Little & Brown, 1991.

Lenore Walker. *The Battered Woman*. Harper & Row, 1979.

David Evan Weiss. *The Great Divide: How Women and Men Really Differ*. Poseidon Press, 1991.

Index